Heir to the Legacy

The Memorable Story of Mike Holmgren's Green Bay Packers

Edited by

FRANCIS J. FITZGERALD

Written by

CHRIS HAVEL, BUD LEA,
THOMAS GEORGE, MICHAEL BAUMAN,
PETE DOUGHERTY, BRAD ZIMANEK
AND TOM SILVERSTEIN

Louisville, Ky.

Acknowledgements

Research Assistance

Lee Remmel, Green Bay Packers; *The Green Bay Press-Gazette*; NFL Properties; Wide World Photo; Allsport Photography USA; Mark Wallenfang Sports Images; Lee Roemer Photography; Brigham Young University; Jim Russ, Alan Whitt, Mike Katz, Craig Yuhas, Ty Halpin and Lori Holladay.

ISBN 1-887761-15-2

Cover and Book Design

David Kordalski, Dale Peskin, and Laura Doolittle
Typefaces: Parkinson Condensed, Village, Berkeley Book

Published By:

AdCraft Sports Marketing
Kaden Tower, 10th Floor
6100 Dutchmans Lane
Louisville, KY 40205
(502) 473-1124

For other sports publications in the AdCraft library, call toll-free (888) 232-7238 or contact our web site at www.sport-mall.com

"Mike Holmgren and his entire staff
have done a miraculous job in Green Bay ....
It is one of the greatest rebuilding
efforts in N.F.L. history."

BILL WALSH
SAN FRANCISCO 49ERS

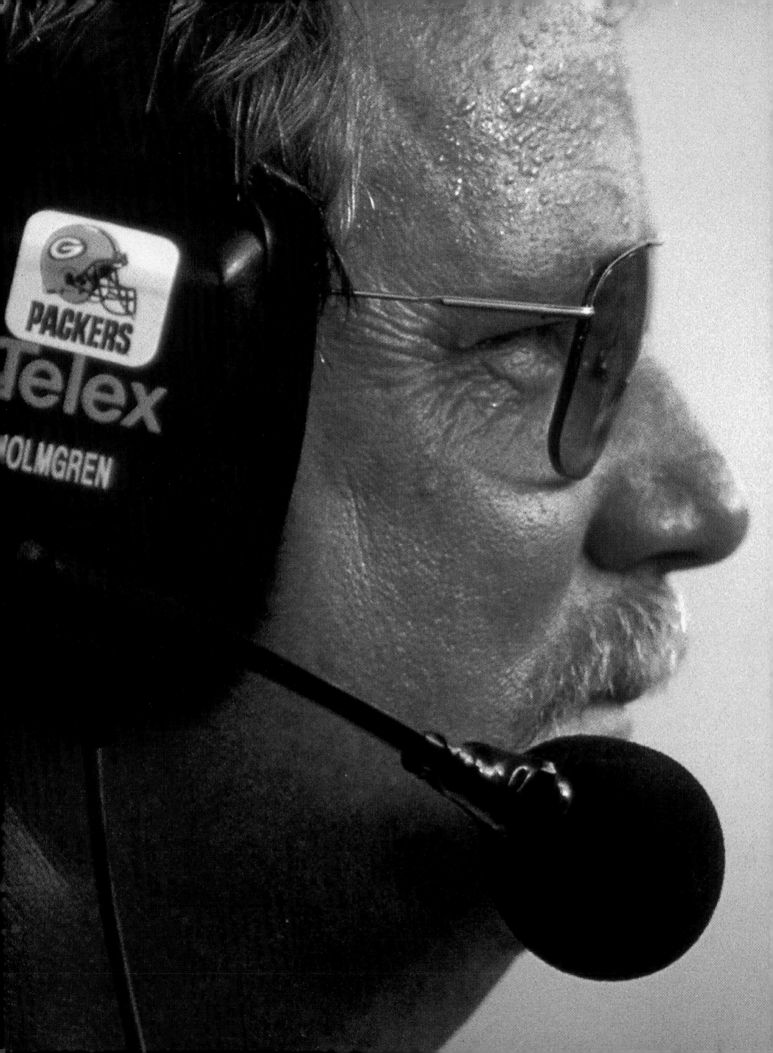

Contents

CHAPTER ONE

A New Era Begins

By Tony Walter

Green Bay Press-Gazette

GREEN BAY, January 11, 1992 — Mike Holmgren looks a little bit like golfer Craig Stadler and feels a lot like actor Robert Redford.

"It was like in that movie years ago, *The Candidate* with Robert Redford," Holmgren said about his initial feelings Friday night when the title of Green Bay Packers head coach became his.

"They pushed him and all of a sudden he gets elected senator and sits down on his bed and they say 'You won.' And he closes the door and he says 'Now what do I do?' But I'm a little more prepared than he was."

Holmgren, 43, was the picture of preparation as he strode into his new job Saturday.

His calm, clear answers. His confident eyes. His navy blue sport coat and gray pants. His sense of humor.

"My feeling was I was hoping my tie was on straight during the whole thing," Holmgren said, when his first Packers press conference ended.

The man selected to be the Packers' 11th head coach brings with him a reputation as a professional, a family man and a teacher.

"You people in Green Bay will love him," said Vic Rowen, the former football coach at San Francisco State who hired Holmgren as an assistant 10 years ago.

Holmgren places his priorities right out on the table.

"Our faith, my family and my work — in that order," he said.

Holmgren and his family — he and his wife, Kathy, have four daughters — are members of the Covenant Church, a Protestant denomination.

Twin daughters Calla and Jenny attend North Park College near Chicago, a small college affiliated with the Covenant Church.

The Holmgrens already are looking for a house in the Green Bay area, and a church.

Behind them, they leave a trail of respect.

"Mike is a people person," said Lynn Stiles, special teams coach for the San Francisco 49ers. "He's a fine coach but he's a finer person. You're getting the best of both worlds with Mike."

"He's a good man to deal with," said John Crumpacker, who covers the 49ers for The San Francisco Examiner. "He's calm and he's agreeable."

Holmgren's reputation for being calm under pressure was observed this past season by reporter Jim Jenkins of The Sacramento Bee when the 49ers' offense sputtered.

"He didn't run and hide," Jenkins said. "He was always willing to talk to reporters, even when they were trying to give him unwanted advice. He's very fair."

Family life apparently hasn't suffered for the Holmgrens, despite the busy schedule of a football coach.

There is a family rule that nobody goes out on Thursday night. Instead, the Holmgrens eat together.

"Mike has things in perspective," Stiles said. "He is able to communicate to people that football isn't a life and death thing."

Holmgren likes to read.

"When I get on airplanes or someplace, I like spy novels, things like that. I might go to non-fiction."

His passion outside of football is golf.

"We had an N.F.L. Alumni golf tournament here and Mike won the long-driving contest with a 287-yard drive," said Art Rosenbaum, the former sports editor of The San Francisco Chronicle. "Mike was complaining because he can't play golf during the season."

Holmgren, who stands 6-5 and weighs 230 pounds, also is a jogger.

Mike Holmgren addresses the media at the press conference announcing his hiring.

CHAPTER TWO

Holmgren: The Early Years

By Chris Havel

Michael George Holmgren is a leader. Green Bay Packers general manager Ron Wolf recognized it fifteen minutes into their first interview on a cold Wisconsin day in January 1992. If Holmgren wanted to be the 11th head coach in Packers history, Wolf decided he couldn't find a better man for the job.

Longtime Brigham Young University head coach LaVell Edwards saw Holmgren's leadership ability, too. He spoke with the young offensive coordinator from San Francisco State for about a half hour. That was all the time he needed to know Holmgren would be his quarterbacks coach, no matter that the young man possessed all of six months college coaching experience.

Steve Ellison, the football coach at Petaluma (Calif.) High, gave Holmgren his first coaching job at San Francisco's Sacred Heart High School. He had a similar experience the first time he met Holmgren.

"He is one of the most personable, down-to-earth people I've ever met," Ellison said. "You meet the guy and it's like you've known him all your life."

Barbara Holmgren smiles when she hears these stories.

It is a mother's pride, of course. But it also is a mother taking delight in knowing that her son's peers see what she has seen almost from the first day

Mike Holmgren began his coaching career at Sacred Heart High School.

he came into her life on June 15, 1948.

"Mike was destined to be a leader from early on," she said. "He was voted traffic patrol leader in grade school. That meant he saw people safely from sidewalk to sidewalk. He always had a way of accepting responsibility. He was an honor student, too. He was everything a mother could hope for in a son."

Holmgren grew up in San Francisco's West Portal area.

Linc Holmgren, his father, operated a Swedish-American bakery and worked as a real estate broker. Barbara worked in the nursing room at San Francisco's Franklin Hospital. Bobbi (Warrington), his oldest sister, is a teacher in Menlo Park, Calif. Calla (Niles), his youngest sister, is an accomplished pianist who resides in Castro Valley, Calif. His brother, Jens, teaches sports to disabled students in San Jose.

The family of six lived in a two story house at 551 Dewey Boulevard in the West Portal neighborhood.

"A large house for large people," Barbara said.

Linc Holmgren stood 6-feet-3 and weighed 330 pounds. Mike, at 6-feet-5 but considerably trimmer, is the tallest coach in Packers history. He is also one of the most athletic, quite a compliment when you consider Bart Starr and Forrest Gregg also coached the Packers.

Mike's love of sports was developed at an early age. Each day, he and his friends would meet at West Portal Park. You name it, they played it. Baseball. Football. Basketball. It didn't matter.

In between games, or on rainy days, Mike and his friends would sneak into The Empire Theater to catch a movie — one of their buddies landed a job there as a manager. Or they would hop into Mike's 57 Olds — affectionately nicknamed 'The Bomber' — and cruise to Lido's delicatessen to grab a sandwich. Or they'd head over to Al's Pizza for a slice of pepperoni and a Coke.

It was an idyllic youth revolving around family, friendship and sports.

One of the first things you learn about San Francisco is that it's surprisingly small for a big city. There were nine high schools when Holmgren was growing up, and many of his best friends didn't attend the same one, but they got to know each other nevertheless.

They'd compete with or against each other in sports during the school year, then hang out together afterward and throughout the summer. Where there was one, you'd find the other. And Mike always seemed to be in the middle of the action. He was the guy who chose up sides, made up the rules, played quarterback, kept everyone in line. He was a terrific organizer, even as a youngster. Beyond that, he was a terrific athlete.

Best friend Bill Jamison said Mike is the only player ever to smack a softball over the fence at West Portal Park.

"And that was about 350 feet," Jamison said. "It was quite a poke."

Holmgren's athletic prowess attained legendary status.

Once, when he was a junior quarterback at San Francisco's Lincoln High, the opposing defense chased him mercilessly. Holmgren had had enough, so instead of drawing up any fancy plays, he turned to his receiver, John Jamison, and said, "Run as far and as fast as you can."

Holmgren took the snap, dropped back and heaved the ball 60 yards in the air, right into the hands of his receiver. Touchdown.

"Everyone who sees that play — I've still got it on film — just gasps," Jamison said. "After that, all the college recruiters started to come around and watch him play."

Growing up in San Francisco, Holmgren wasn't just a good passer. He was a great passer.

"The best high school quarterback I ever saw," said Dan Fouts, a Hall of Fame quarterback who starred with the San Diego Chargers.

Holmgren went on to be named California's Senior Athlete of the Year. He also started for the North in the Shrine All-Star Game in Los Angeles, where he beat out another hotshot passer from the Bay area. That other quarterback's name: Jim Plunkett.

Naturally, the recruiters swarmed. They included the University of Southern California's head coach, John McKay, and the defensive coordinator from Brigham Young, an ambitious young fellow by the name of LaVell Edwards.

Holmgren accepted a scholarship to U.S.C. in 1965, leaving Edwards to say, "When I interviewed Mike (in 1982) and he took the job, I told him, After all these years, I finally got you to come to Provo."

Edwards can only wonder at what records Holmgren may have set at pass-oriented Brigham Young.

"He was big. He was strong. He could throw the football," Edwards said. "I think he'd have played for us. And I think he'd have been very good."

Holmgren's decision to sign with U.S.C. would've been a wise one, except McKay never really warmed up to the idea of having a true drop-back passer in the lineup. Holmgren, at 6-5 and 220 lbs., had a powerful and accurate arm, but he lacked the quick feet McKay coveted.

So Holmgren was forced to sit behind Steve Sogge for two seasons and Jimmy Jones for another. He completed 8 of 27 passes for 108 yards, one touchdown and one interception in limited time with the Trojans. He missed his senior season with a knee injury.

Still, he had a way of making an impression.

Andy Reid, a wide-eyed kid from Los Angeles, recalls sneaking into the Trojans' game and being amazed at Holmgren's arm strength, even though he rarely played. Today, Reid coaches the tight ends for Holmgren and the Packers.

"I was the biggest U.S.C. fan in the world," Reid said. "I'd go to all the games and I knew about Mike back then. He was a classic drop-back passer with a great arm. He just never really got the chance to play."

Hall of Fame running back O.J. Simpson, who teamed with Holmgren at U.S.C., thought the strong-armed quarterback would be the Trojans' starter when he signed there.

"When we first got there, all of us thought Holmgren was going to be 'The Man,' " Simpson said. "But Sogge was great at audibilizing at the line of scrimmage and McKay loved that. If it hadn't been for Sogge's ability to audibilize, there's no telling how great Holmgren might have been."

As it turned out, not only did Holmgren not play at U.S.C., he didn't even letter.

Holmgren appreciated Simpson's compliment. The two played against each other in high school and became friends at U.S.C.

"My claim to fame," said Holmgren, "is tackling Simpson after I threw an interception. I remember joking about it years later when I'd see O.J. running. I'd say, 'Geez, it can't be that hard to tackle him.' "

To his credit, Holmgren never grew bitter over his lack of playing time at U.S.C.

"It was really hard to accept, as you might expect," he admitted. "But I got a fine education there and tried to handle it as best I could."

Although Holmgren seldom played for the Trojans, he was drafted in the eighth round by the St. Louis Cardinals. He survived until the final cut, and then was left to decide what to do.

It wasn't an easy time in his life. His father, Linc, experienced the first of several heart attacks.

Holmgren remembers driving "a million miles an hour" to get him to the hospital. Unfortunately, there

Holmgren explains an opposing team's defense to B.Y.U. quarterback Robbie Bosco during a timeout in 1984.

was nothing he could do when Linc's third heart attack came. It claimed him at 48.

Mike assumed the responsibility of taking his mother to get her driver's license and teaching her about balancing checkbooks and so forth. Meantime, he had to sort out what he was going to do to make a living because he and his high school sweetheart, Kathy, had just gotten married.

A friend suggested Mike try being a substitute teacher and assistant football coach at Sacred Heart High School in San Francisco, Mike embraced the idea. Kathy tells the story of how proud Mike was to be getting $300 to coach, only to realize it was $300 for the entire season, not each month.

"We were so naive," she said, still able to smile.

Two years and 24 losses later at Sacred Heart, Holmgren's enthusiasm for coaching hadn't dwindled, although it taught him a valuable lesson.

Said Ellison, "That experience was really useful to both of us. We were young coaches and I think it gave us a good perspective. We learned you need good players to win."

Holmgren also learned the value of self-control, a quality that was reinforced under the incredibly even-tempered Edwards at B.Y.U. His Sacred Heart team played marvelously against the San Jose powerhouse Mitty High, which was expected to win by 50 points. But Holmgren's team played with enough guts to trail only 7-0 at halftime. In fact, Sacred Heart should've won, except several offensive miscues got Mitty High two touchdowns.

"I was so proud of our guys, I was almost in tears walking into the locker room," Ellison said. "We get in there and Mike is so mad we're behind, he punches the chalkboard and starts yelling, which is out of character."

Eventually, the team filed out for the second half and as he was leaving, Ellison heard Holmgren let out with a blood-curdling scream.

"I thought he died," Ellison said. "It turns out he hurt his hand real bad hitting the chalkboard, but he didn't want to let on to the team. We just looked at each other and started laughing."

Holmgren's coaching career led him to San Jose's Oak Grove High School, where he was offensive coordinator and quarterbacks coach from 1975-80. Phil Stearns, the head coach there, gave Holmgren the freedom to run the offense. Holmgren's star quarterback was a kid by the name of Marty Mornhinweg, who started as a sophomore and went on to be a four-year letterwinner at the University of Montana.

Mornhinweg currently is Holmgren's quarterbacks coach with the Packers.

"He taught me the basic fundamentals of playing the quarterback position," Mornhinweg said. "I think his involvement meant everything to my success. He's also probably the single greatest reason I went into coaching."

Mornhinweg said Holmgren seemed entirely content being a high school history teacher and assistant football coach. He said the two never discussed his coaching aspirations.

"It surprised me when he made the move to San Francisco State," Mornhinweg said. "What doesn't surprise me one bit is how successful he's been since then. He was my first coach. I guess I didn't know how fortunate I was to play for a guy like Mike

Holmgren and the rest of that staff at Oak Grove until really I was done playing and into coaching.

"Mike can make anybody, whether it be a staff member of a player or a support staff person, and make them feel like they're wanted, needed and doing a great job. He can get the most out of you. That's a special quality he has. When he talks to you one-on-one, even as a group, he gets his point across."

Holmgren finally left Oak Grove to be the offensive coordinator at San Francisco State in 1981. Six months later, State's head coach, Vic Rowen, recommended Holmgren to his close friend at Brigham Young, LaVell Edwards.

If Edwards was skeptical about Holmgren's lack of coaching experience at the college level, they were eased 10 minutes into his interview.

"He was very personable to begin with," Edwards said. "He hadn't had a lot of experience, he'd been at San Francisco State for one season, about six months. But he came very highly recommended by Vic Rowen, who I had a great deal of regard for. I was very impressed with Mike. He had a good knowledge of game. He was a good worker. Frankly, he did an outstanding job for us."

It was at B.Y.U. that Holmgren met Steve Young, who would go on to be a Super Bowl m.v.p. quarterback with the San Francisco 49ers. Young arrived at B.Y.U. as an option quarterback from Greenwich (Connecticut) High. Under Holmgren's tutelage, Young went on to become a complete quarterback.

"Steve had great talent and ability, but he needed refinement," Edwards said. "Mike taught him the value of patience and waiting for things to unfold. With guys like Steve, who are excellent runners, there's always that tendency to pull it down and take off at the least little thing. Steve wasn't too bad that way, and under Mike, he really blossomed."

Young has many fond memories of Holmgren, even though the coach had to walk a tightrope at

As an assistant with the 49ers, Holmgren tutored quarterbacks Steve Bono (left) and Joe Montana (right).

San Francisco when Young and Joe Montana were both there.

"Mike is one of the best coaches ever because he understands people," Young said. "He can sit down and have a conversation with somebody and know what kind of football player they are. A lot of people measure it by speed and how far you can jump. Things that are just objective. He's the kind of guy that can get subjective with his personalities. He can put a team together that's going to play hard.

"And then I think he's one of the greatest coaches in out-coaching the other coach," Young added. "He

can put a game plan together and attack it and adjust. He's phenomenal."

Holmgren, who also coached record-setting passer Robbie Bosco at B.Y.U., helped the Cougars win a national championship in 1984. His affable nature made him an effective, valued recruiter, as well.

Reid, who was an offensive guard and later a graduate assistant at B.Y.U., was on the staff when Holmgren arrived. He said it was immediately clear that Holmgren had a keen, well-developed grasp of the passing game.

"A lot of guys come in with not a lot of college coaching experience, but he was very advanced," Reid said. "I was measuring him against those other guys, and they were good, but this guy (Holmgren) was good, too. This guy was going somewhere."

Reid proved prophetic.

In 1986, San Francisco 49ers coach Bill Walsh called for Edwards' permission to offer Holmgren the job as quarterbacks coach. Edwards obliged and Holmgren accepted.

The move united Holmgren and Joe Montana, one of the N.F.L.'s greatest quarterbacks of all time, and the duo proved deadly to opposing N.F.L. defenses. It also enabled Holmgren to learn from Walsh, a man he considers one of the finest coaches in N.F.L. history.

"I think," Holmgren said, "if you could combine the qualities of LaVell Edwards and Bill Walsh, you might just have the perfect football coach. LaVell was so even-tempered, so organized, so morally proper. And Bill was such a perfectionist and perhaps the most successful offensive coach ever. Well, I just hope I've learned from both of them."

Walsh remembers wanting to include Holmgren's name on a list of candidates for the 49ers' quarterbacks coach job in 1986.

"There were some really high-powered guys on that list, but I wanted to include Mike because I'd known him at Oak Grove High, I'd known him up at San Francisco State and at B.Y.U.

"Well, we want through a series of interviews and it was easy for me to decide on Mike. He was excellent expressing himself. He had an excellent grasp of fundamental football. He had a personality where you could deal comfortably with him. He had a style and a persona that was very impressive. He just fit right in with the style of coaching we did."

Through Holmgren's first two seasons with the 49ers, they went 10-5-1 in 1986 and 13-2 in 1987, but each time were bounced out in their first playoff game, In 1988, the 49ers had no intention of coming up short, and it was this year that Holmgren stepped into the limelight.

Dennis Green, then the 49ers' receivers coach, was named head coach at Stanford late in the 1988

Packer coaches – First 4 Years
Percent of Games Won

Vince Lombardi (39-13)	75.0
Curly Lambeau (21-11-5)	63.5
Mike Holmgren (42-29)	**59.2**
Phil Bengston[1] (20-21-1)	48.8
Dan Devine (25-28-4)	47.4
Forrest Gregg (25-37-1)	40.5
Lindy Infante (24-40)	37.5
Bart Starr (21-36-1)	37.1
Lisle Blackburn (17-31)	35.4
Gene Ronzani (14-31-1)	31.5
"Scooter" McLean[2] (1-10-1)	12.5

1 - Coached 3 years, 2 - Coached 1 year

season. San Francisco was struggling at 6-5 when Green made the announcement. Walsh, realizing that it would be difficult for Green to stay on top of things at both places, asked Holmgren to assume more responsibility.

"Really, once you're sort of an absentee coach, you're gone," Walsh said. "Denny was there and Denny wanted to help me, but his mind was elsewhere, so I turned to Mike to help me with the offense. He just did a great job. He stepped right forward. So at that point I knew there was a real future, not only with the 49ers, but elsewhere for Mike."

The 49ers went on to defeat Cincinnati, 20-16, in Super Bowl XXIII and Walsh retired. One of the first things his replacement, George Seifert, did was name Holmgren offensive coordinator.

The result was a more varied and versatile 49ers attack. Future Hall of Fame quarterback Joe Montana would have the best season of his career, with an N.F.L. single-season record 112.4 passing rating. He threw a career-low eight interceptions under Holmgren's tutelage.

Holmgren always described himself as the caretaker of Walsh's offense, though he made some perceptible, subtle changes in 1989. He utilized fullback Tom Rathman, primarily a blocker in past seasons, as a go-to receiver. He implemented a three-tight end alignment to help beef up the running game. He also paid more attention to the gifted John Taylor opposite Jerry Rice. Taylor developed into a Pro Bowl receiver and took a lot of pressure off Rice.

San Francisco marched through the playoffs en route to a 55-10 victory over Denver in Super Bowl XXIV.

Despite the pressure of filling in for Green, Holmgren had a knack for staying upbeat and loose, characteristics the 49ers offensive players fed off.

"He's a hilarious guy," Young said. "He's always straight with you. He never wants the mood to be somber or down no matter what. But he really gets mad a lot. He doesn't scream. He'll hold it in. It builds in his neck, so his neck actually bulges out. He's got a big neck as it is. There was one time in college I remember he wanted to talk to me after a time-out. He was just furious with me. I called timeout. He says, 'Get over here!' I go, 'I won't go over until you calm down.' That made him even more mad."

Young still laughs at Holmgren's sense of humor.

"For a football coach, he's very unusual," Young said. "To me that's a real compliment because so many times we get these stoic, non-people people coaching the ultimate people sport. If you're not good with people in football, then you're really five yards behind the line. That's why you notice, the teams that do well year in and year out, are coached by people who understand people such as (Pittsburgh's) Bill Cowher or (Washington's) Norv Turner. It's because they're communicating well. Mike has this tremendous knack for it. Plus, he's a

lot of fun."

Perhaps Holmgren's finest coaching job came in 1991, his last season with the 49ers. Montana was out with a back injury and Young missed six games with a knee injury, leaving the offense in the hands of third-string quarterback Steve Bono.

Holmgren stayed with Bono and the two coaxed six straight victories out of San Francisco and an improbable 10-6 record. They narrowly missed the playoffs that season.

"I owe Steve Bono a great thanks," Holmgren said. "That last year we were together, he played the last six games for the 49ers and we won six games in a row. No one thought we'd do that. We were struggling a little bit.

"One of the (San Francisco) columnists referred to me as brain-dead, affectionately, of course. And here we are with the third-string quarterback and going good. The team responded and Steve responded beautifully.

"That allowed me to get back into the mind of Ron Wolf or someone who thought I could coach a little bit. I've always said that about Steve. I helped him a little bit. I owed him a great deal."

A month later, Wolf called seeking permission to talk to Holmgren. The 49ers obliged, though they got a 1992 fourth-round draft pick from the Packers in return for Holmgren. It turned out to be a steal.

"I think originally (Holmgren) expected to return to college football and be a head coach, like most of us did. But when the team then went ahead and won the Super Bowl the year after I retired and he was a major factor in the coordinating job, it was self-evident he would be an N.F.L. head coach," Walsh said. "He had opportunities that year and other years and he was just fortunate, as I was, that he got with the right organization because Ron Wolf's an excellent executive and Green Bay's an excellent opportunity. Everything fit into place for him to do that."

CHAPTER THREE

West Coast Offense Comes to the Dairyland

By Brad Zimanek

On the morning of Sunday, Jan. 12, 1992, the front page headline of The Green Bay Press-Gazette blared: "What Makes Mike Tick?"

Rumors of the hiring of Mike Holmgren as the new coach of the Green Bay Packers were floating around since his interview two weeks earlier, and the city's faithful fans wanted to know as much as possible about the man that was going to attempt to lead the home team from the N.F.L.'s gallows.

Some of the vital statistics revealed:

First, Holmgren and his family — consisting of his wife, Kathy, and four daughters — are members of the Covenant Church, a Protestant denomination. At the time, his twin daughters, Calla and Jenny, were attending their mother's alma mater of North Park (Ill.) College, which is affiliated with the church.

Second, the former high school history teacher planned on buying a home soon. The family quickly settled on a modest abode (by the standards of an N.F.L. head coach) a few miles from Lambeau Field.

Third, family is very important to Holmgren. Even during the busy schedule of a football season filled with long hours, Thursday evenings are reserved for eating together.

Other tidbits uncovered later were that Holmgren always desired to be a rock star, watches *Seinfeld* and

As the World Turns, wears a leather jacket when riding his Harley-Davidson motorcycle, and likes to listen to country music stars Vince Gill and Garth Brooks.

What wasn't revealed was how Holmgren, who strongly resembled PGA golfer Craig Stadler and who had never been a head coach before at any level, was going to fare under one of the most difficult challenges in sports — rebuilding a downtrodden team basically from the ground up.

Holmgren acknowledged as such in his opening press conference when he said: "It was like in that movie years ago, *The Candidate* with Robert Redford. They pushed him and all of a sudden he gets elected senator and sits down on his bed and they say, 'You won!' And he closes the door and he says, 'Now what do I do?' But I'm a little more prepared than he was."

That was evident throughout the organization almost from Day One.

Longtime Packer public relations director Lee Remmel — who has been involved with the coverage of the Packers through every one of the team's coaching regimes dating back to founder Curly Lambeau in the mid-1940's — said that was one aspect of Holmgren that was not difficult to detect.

Mike Holmgren visits with quarterback Brett Favre during a timeout.

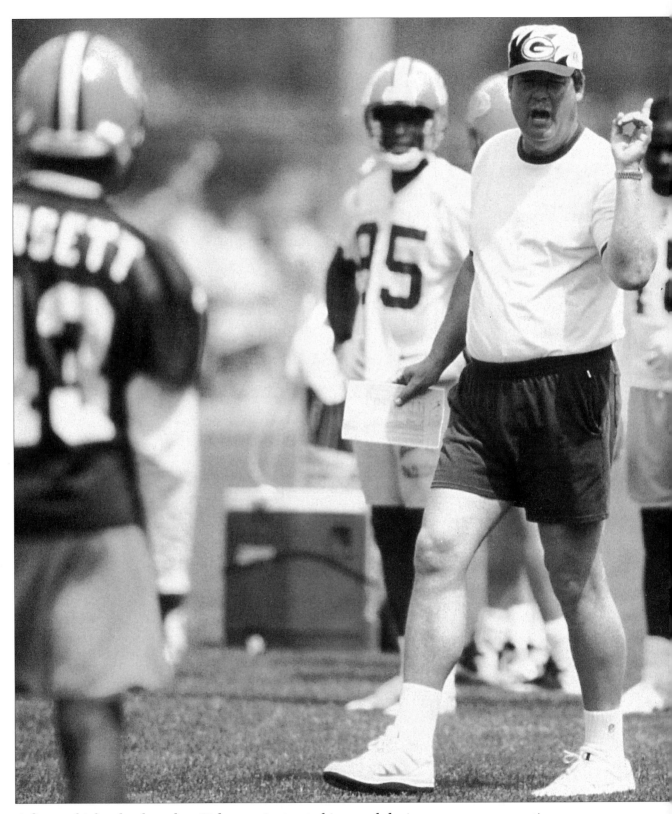

A former high school teacher, Holmgren instructs his squad during a preseason practice.

"He had an exact idea of where he was going and how to get there," Remmel said. "And that impression has been strongly reinforced. Gil Haskell, one of the assistant coaches, said that Holmgren had been preparing himself for a long time to become a head coach in the N.F.L. and I think it showed."

The first thing Holmgren needed to attend to was changing the mind-set in the locker room and throughout the community in general.

"You had to battle an attitude as much as anything," Holmgren said. "They had lost a lot of close games in the fourth quarter and for a number of years. They had a fine season in 1989, but most of the time they had been either average or they lost. And the players that were here — the standard of play that they think is good enough, isn't. So you have to establish a new standard. That was the biggest thing. Trying to evaluate players and be fair with the guys. You come in and you had to release a lot of guys and start fresh."

And with the help of general manager Ron Wolf, Holmgren has led the Packers to four straight winning seasons when Green Bay only had five from 1968 to 1991. Holmgren believes turning a team around is not as difficult as it appears if the proper management is in place and the correct decisions are made.

"I don't think it should be hard, especially in professional football as opposed to college football," Holmgren said. "In college, maybe you are in a conference that other teams have better facilities and you don't really have a level playing field, so recruiting is harder.

"But at the professional level the draft is set up so the poorer teams get a better position. You have free agency. You have an opportunity to trade, if you evaluate personnel correctly. So there are ways to get better. You have to have a team and management, and in my case, Ron (Wolf), that will hang in there

Above: With a keen eye for details, Holmgren observes a practice drill.

Right: Holmgren pleads his case for a first down with the officials.

with you through some bumps and tough times. And they are committed to your way of doing things, as well. Then you have to make good personnel decisions. You can't make a lot of mistakes. Everyone makes mistakes. It happens. It's part of our game. You are not going to hit on everyone in the draft. No one does. But you can't make too many."

Holmgren's reputation as an offensive genius is what preceded him to Green Bay, and was the primary reason for his half-dozen head coaching interviews throughout the league following the 1991 season. That raised a red flag to many Packers fans at the time.

The team had just finished a four-year, 24-40 stint with Lindy Infante (now the head coach of the

Indianapolis Colts) that was highlighted by a woeful inability to run the football. Many said that Holmgren and Infante were similar in their pass-happy offensive philosophies, but Wolf, who was the driving force in Holmgren's hiring, begged to differ.

"The difference between the two is Mike's success running the ball," Wolf said. "We talked about that quite a bit."

A potent ground game — proven as a key ingredient in taking a team to the Super Bowl, as every winner the last decade has finished in the top 10 in rushing — has been an evolving process in the Packers' version of the West Coast offense.

Holmgren's desire to mount a consistent ground attack didn't immediately match the personnel he acquired from a team that finished 4-12 the previous season. So he improvised with the help of the screen pass.

Ex-49ers coach Bill Walsh, who installed the West Coast offense for the first time with San Francisco in 1979, where it went on to help win five Super Bowls, was not fond of the screen. In Walsh's mind, screens opened up rushing lanes that increased the chance of the defense getting to the quarterback.

But Holmgren did not have a bruising fullback such as Tom Rathman or a powerful halfback such as Roger Craig like the 49ers did when Holmgren served as the team's quarterbacks coach and, later, offensive coordinator.

"They weren't able to run the ball at Green Bay like San Francisco could," said then-Minnesota defensive coordinator and current Tampa Bay coach Tony Dungy. "So how do you take pressure off of the passing game? You go to the screen to slow people down."

And it worked with incredible success early in Holmgren's tenure.

"They're the best screen team in the history of

football; the best I've ever seen," said one-time Packers assistant Jon Gruden, who is now the offensive coordinator for the Philadelphia Eagles.

Edgar Bennett, who played fullback for two years before switching to halfback in 1995, was the key ingredient, catching 78 passes in 1994, a franchise record for receptions by a running back.

"It was another weapon and a way to get the ball into the backs' hands and get the lineman out in

At the Pro Bowl, Holmgren chats with his two great quarterbacks, Steve Young of the 49ers, and Brett Favre.

front of them,'" says Sherman Lewis, Holmgren's offensive coordinator since 1992. "It wasn't that complicated. It was another part of our run game, really."

But Holmgren continued to adapt as the team upgraded its talent level, beginning with the selection of fullback William Henderson, a 250-pounder out of North Carolina who Lewis calls "really a big, blocking guard."

In 1995, Bennett, behind the blocking of Henderson and running back Dorsey Levens, began an assault on the 1,000-yard rushing mark that had not been attained by a Packer since Terdell Middleton in 1978.

Bennett did eclipse the number in the 15th game, albeit with a rather pedestrian yards-per-carry average. Holmgren joked that it was one of the crowning achievements of his life, considering how often he was peppered by the media for the lack of a running game.

However, the tone was set early in the 1996 season when a healthier Bennett was on pace to reach the same figure with much fewer attempts.

"It's important," Holmgren said. "You are not going to go as far as you would like to go without a running game. I know that. You need balance. The passing game helps set up the run here; I believe that. Some teams do it the other way. But the passing game here sets up the run and people play a little softer defending the pass and thinking a lot about the pass and it allows you to run the ball."

The basic components of the West Coast offense are an intelligent — though not necessarily rocket-armed — quarterback, two physical receivers, a tight end equally adept at blocking and receiving, a powerful fullback and a versatile halfback. The premise of the offense — whose pieces are now in place not only in Green Bay, but Minnesota, Denver, Kansas City and Philadelphia, among others — is fairly simple: quick precision.

"People are trying to find ways to stop this offense and the bottom line is the only way we are stopped is if we stop ourselves," Packers quarterback Brett Favre says. "You can execute this offense against any defense if you just be patient and do what basically what you are coached to do. I think that's where we are a lot better."

The quick routes and passes put the balls into the hands of the receivers where they are asked to gain yardage after the catch. The quarterback uses primarily three- and five-step drops to reduce the possibility for sacks and short patterns cut down on a defender's opportunity for interception.

"It's a high-percentage offense," says Green Bay defensive assistant Johnny Holland, who was also a starting linebacker and the leading tackler on Holmgren's first Packer team. "It's not a lot of deep balls thrown and lucky plays. The quarterback knows where the guys are going to be. It doesn't come overnight. I remember Brett Favre's first year running this offense and he found it pretty complicated.

"I also remember playing the 49ers and Joe

During the spring and summer, Holmgren is often seen riding his Harley-Davidson.

Montana completed like 19 of 20 passes. That's what this offense is all about — ball control and not making mistakes. That's one reason as a coach why Mike plays attention to the fine details because that's what it takes for the offense to work."

The passing game uses a series of triangles where receivers run complimentary patterns. The flood of three receivers (a running back, tight end and split end) into an area of a defensive zone consisting of two players means the defenders must decide whom to cover. A quarterback reads what the defenders are doing and throws the ball to the player left unattended.

It can be very frustrating to a defender — even some Packers players who have gone up against the offense the last five years in practice.

Vince Lombardi set the standard for all Packers' coaches.

CHAPTER FOUR

Taming the Legend that Haunts

By Thomas George

Phil Bengston, Dan Devine, Bart Starr, Forrest Gregg and Lindy Infante all tried. Each traveled to Green Bay to become head coach of the fabled Packers, the Curly Lambeau Packers, the wondrous Packers, the wondrous franchise with those 11 world championships.

Once Lombardi left after the 1967 season, each of these five men in succession came to Green Bay and each soon went. Each tried to match Lombardi's sparkling record of 98-30-4 and his victories in Super Bowls I and II. None of the five, however, was able to muster even a .500 record in Green Bay.

Ron Wolf, the Packers general manager, arrived in Green Bay on Nov. 27, 1991. Fewer than two months later, Mike Holmgren was Wolf's selection as Packers coach. Holmgren was next in line — now it was his turn to attempt to tame the legend that haunts.

"First and foremost, I respected the job that Mike had done in San Francisco as offensive coordinator," said Wolf, "because he had resurrected the careers of some very average players. I had come up in a defensive system and initially I wanted a defensive-minded head coach. But then I thought about it, and I said, 'Hey, when you look at the guys who took over during the 80's — Reeves and Gibbs and Walsh and some others — most of them were offensive-minded guys.' That turned my thought-process around. That

peaked my curiosity toward Mike."

Once Wolf met him, he saw qualities that he admired. He liked the way that Holmgren was a fan of football and how he represented the game. He liked his calm, even personality.

"Once I met him, in the first 15 minutes, I knew this was the guy," Wolf said.

The coach that could tame the legend that haunts.

"It wasn't an easy sell," Wolf said. "I mean, it was like this guy was on some sort of tour. There were at least six other National Football League teams that wanted him. It was like he was the girl with the curls. We got lucky."

Indeed.

Because Mike Holmgren is doing it. This is his fifth season in Green Bay as head coach and his records have been: 9-7 in 1992; 9-7 in 1993; 9-7 in 1994; 11-5 in 1995 and eight victories in his first nine games in the 1996 season. He won the National Football Conference Central Division title last season and the Packers had not done that in 23 years. He has led Green Bay to the playoffs in each of the last three seasons and that had not happened in Green Bay since Lombardi seasons of '65, '66 and '67.

His eighth win of this season at that juncture gave him a 50-30 record in Green Bay. That gave the Packers 12 straight wins and — get this — at that point gave Holmgren a 24-4 record in Lambeau, bet-

ter than Lombardi's record (23-5) in his first 28 games there.

Cool it now, Holmgren says. No applause.

"There never will be another Coach Lombardi," he recently told *Gameday* magazine. "I don't think anyone will ever be able to duplicate his success. I don't hear voices or see ghosts or any of those things. And I don't dwell on the comparisons. I just have to be myself and do the best I can."

His best has been quite good.

How has he done it?

Well, he and Wolf make an excellent team. Wolf's job is to obtain the talent and Holmgren's job is to coach it. Both have excelled in each of their responsibilities.

Holmgren has hired knowledgeable, superior coaches as assistants, including offensive coordinator Sherman Lewis and Fritz Shurmur. He has stayed close to what he knows best — offense — and he has developed solid working relationships with his players.

"His style is probably the closest, along with Ray Rhodes and Denny Green, to mine; his offensive philosophies parallel mine," said Bill Walsh, whom Holmgren worked for in San Fransisco. "There are those who say right now that he is the best coach in football. He is right there with the best coaches in the N.F.L. today. He is smart. He has a great football mind. His style with people makes them feel comfortable around them. He has charisma and he is easy going but there is a bottom line; there is a point where he can be resistant.

"He and Ron Wolf also do a great job of finding, acquiring, developing and utilizing talent. Some can do one or two of these things but few can do them

Curly Lambeau visits with his two stars, Don Hutson (left) and Irv Comp (right).

all like they do. Mike is just a complete coach."

Still, Holmgren has had to learn on the job. He has made adjustments in his own philosophies and temperment. Take his relationship with his quarterback, Brett Farve, for example.

Holmgren views himself as orderly, controlled emotion and tirelessly prepared. Favre is more unorthodox, a scrambler, a gunslinger. Initially, those two clashed.

"He (Holmgren) would insist that something had to be done this way, exactly this way, and I guess I would sort of rebel," Favre later recalled. "I mean, I would listen, I would try it, but some things I really thought, for me, would be better if I did them my way. He didn't buy that — at first."

Holmgren, however, saw that he had to give.

"It got to the point where I was on him so much that he was not getting any room to grow," Holmgren said. "I was so tough on him that I was squeezing the spark out of him, the special trait that he has that makes him a special quarterback. I saw that I had to give. After a while, I told Brett he was my quarterback and that together we were either going to sink or swim. But the one thing was, either way, we were going to do it together."

Smart move. Favre threw 38 touchdown passes last season and won N.F.L. most valuable player honors. This season he has picked up where he left off, scrambling, sliding in the pocket to create more time, finding open receivers and lifting Green Bay's offense to new heights.

"Brett had to mature — you can only be so free a spirit," Walsh said. "Mike had to learn about him and he has. Mike heavily depends on Favre's ability to play the field. He moves and finds people and throws the ball and Mike allows him to do that. Now, that can hurt you. In our game against them up there, Favre threw an interception that almost lost the game for them. But then, he came back, and

I was suprised because we do have one heck of a defense."

Holmgren, who is from the Bay Area, beat his old team, the 49ers, on ABC's Monday Night Game of the Week on Oct. 14th in a thrilling 23-20 overtime game at Lambeau Field. That victory followed a 27-17 playoff victory for Holmgren and the Packers last January in San Franscisco.

"You could tell how much that game meant to him, said Packers defensive end Sean Jones. "He was excited, a little more than we are used to seeing him get excited. He was especially focused during the week — we all were because it was a playoff game — and once it was over, you could tell what it meant to all of us but especially to him."

Reggie White, the Packers all-pro defensive end, said of Holmgren: "Mike is honest and he sets a tone that lets players know that he cares about winning and he cares about you. He can dictate the flow of the game with his play-calling. He gets people prepared. We have a lot of respect for him around here."

Taming the legend that haunts? Holmgren is quite close, Walsh says.

"I think they will win a world championship at some point but I hope it's not this year because we want to win it," said Walsh, who has returned to the 49ers as an administrative assistant. "Mike and his entire staff has done a miraculous job in Green Bay.

"When you think about the talent and the players that they have and that those players would be willing to go and live in Green Bay, in a nice town, but one that is isolated with brutal weather, to think they could get free agents and a team like they have there, it is one of the great rebuilding efforts in N.F.L. history. I know if I was there every day — and I'm from California — and it's December and the wind off that

Curly Lambeau, the winningest coach in Packers history with a 212-106-21 record.

The Packers defeated Dallas, 21-17, in the famous Ice Bowl in 1967.

Lombardi watches his team from the sideline in Super Bowl I.

water starts blasting you, well, I'd be wondering, 'What in the heck I'm doing here?'"

In Green Bay, there is plenty of old history. The Packers are looking for new history.

"Mike communicates well with his staff and with the players and that is important because football today is a whole new system," Wolf said. "With free agency and how you build your team today, you must have that. I think the key is that nobody here has a different agenda. Mike and everybody's agenda here is the same and that is for the Packers to once again be champions."

That, for certain, is the best way for Holmgren to tame the legend that haunts.

CHAPTER FIVE

Always a Winner

By Tom Silverstein

Mike Holmgren was a winner long before he walked through the dark, hallowed tunnel that leads to Lambeau Field for the first time.

He had been a winner at every level in the game of football — as a high school and college quarterback, as a high school coach, as a college assistant coach, and as quarterbacks coach and offensive coordinator with the San Francisco 49ers.

With a resume like that, it was hard to believe there were doubts that he could turn the Green Bay Packers into a winner.

But when Holmgren became the organization's 11th head coach on January 11, 1992, he was inheriting a rag-tag group that knew as much about winning as a novice blackjack player. Of the 53 players with whom he started the 1992 season, only three had ever played in a playoff game with the Packers.

Losing ran through every crack and crevice of the Packers psyche, from the front office to the equipment staff. Since legendary coach Vince Lombardi turned in his clipboard after Super Bowl II, the Packers had experienced winning seasons just five times in 24 seasons.

That Holmgren has been able to forge such a pointed attack against human nature — turning a 4-12 team into a 9-7 squad and posting winning seasons in each of his seasons in Green Bay — is a testament to his style. He has not only turned the Packers into winners on paper, but in their minds as well.

"The credit for that goes to Mike Holmgren and his staff," Packers general manager Ron Wolf said. "They have done a magnificent job of changing an attitude and a perception here of what the Packers are all about. Not only on the field, but off the field as well.

"People throughout the league no longer look at Green Bay as 'The Frozen Tundra.' They look at it as a great place to play football."

Of course, Wolf has had a great deal to do with it, supplying Holmgren with the materials to create a perennial winner, but it is Holmgren who has molded the clay into his own personal masterpiece. He has drawn upon his many experiences to guide the Packers through their evolution from also-rans to Super Bowl contenders.

In the same way the Packers matured from their days of blunder, Holmgren has grown also. Every season has presented new challenges, and every season he has come up with new ways to attack them.

What has also remained a constant has been Holmgren's attention to detail, something he brought with him from his earliest days in football. He insists in having a hand in everything — from personally coaching the quarterbacks to setting up *soul-food catering* for the players — mostly because if it's not done right, he would kick himself later for not having done it on his own.

"What impressed me most about Mike when I interviewed him was how detailed he was about B.Y.U.'s offense," said Bill Walsh, who hired Holmgren from Brigham Young in 1986 to be his

Mike Holmgren studies the progress of his offense from the sideline.

quarterbacks coach. "When I noted that, I thought that he was someone I could hire. He had an attention to detail and a football mind. I was really impressed with his administrative and leadership qualities."

When Holmgren arrived in Green Bay, his biggest concern was integrating his offensive and defensive systems, but there were other fish to fry. Like uniting a group of players who had been divided by losing, and eliminating a climate of fear and uncertainty created by displaced Packers coach Lindy Infante.

Nowhere was the problem more prevalent than on the offensive line, where selfishness and egos had split the ranks. Holmgren and offensive line coach Tom Lovat moved quickly to lay down the law.

"When he came in, our offensive line probably typified the regression of this team," said tackle Ken Ruettgers, who is in his 12th season with the team. "There were pride and ego problems, there were split factions that were at war with each other. It was just not a real positive place to come to work everyday.

"I think anytime there's a change with coaches or upstairs, it's almost like there's a clean slate. And then I think Coach Lovat and Ron and Mike listened to the players about what was going on. I think Tom laid down the law and met it face-to-face, which is what needed to be done. Mike is pro-respect and pro-honor for one another. There was a lot of that lacking when he got here."

To date, Holmgren does not tolerate selfishness among his troops. The list of players who have been called into his office because they've complained to the media about lack of playing time or displeasure with the system is long and glorious.

One of Holmgren's favorite targets is strong safety LeRoy Butler, who is a vocal leader on the team and one of the best interviews in the locker room. Butler has been called onto the carpet so many

Reggie White discusses defensive strategy with Holmgren at practice.

times, he automatically checks in at the front door to see if Holmgren wants to see him.

Still, Butler plays hard for Holmgren. He is one of the coach's favorite players because he is honest, hard-working and a decent human being.

The caliber of assistant coaches that Holmgren brought in has also been key to his success in Green Bay. Perhaps reflecting the knack Walsh had for hiring talented assistants who would someday be head coaches, Holmgren has assembled a solid staff.

Since he's been in Green Bay, two of his assistants have landed head coaching jobs and another was a finalist for a head position. Defensive coordinator Ray Rhodes now coaches the Philadelphia Eagles, quarterbacks coach Steve Mariucci coaches at the University of California, and offensive coordinator Sherman Lewis was a finalist for the Michigan State job several years ago.

Holmgren has the final say on everything — perhaps on too many things — but he does allow his coaches tremendous input on game-plans and personnel. For instance, Lewis, Lovat, tight ends coach Andy Reid, receivers coach Gil Haskell and running

backs coach Harry Sydney all come up with a list of plays they like against each week's opponent. Holmgren then goes through the list and picks the ones he feels most comfortable with.

At the end of the season, Holmgren has two of his assistants do an evaluation of the job he has done.

One of the things Holmgren believes is critical to creating team chemistry is fostering a pleasant atmosphere in which to go to work. A family-oriented man himself, Holmgren shows special concern for his players.

"We've tried very hard to create an atmosphere where a player would enjoy playing here and want to be here," Holmgren said. "To what do we attribute that to? I don't know. We work very hard at it. I really personally believe it helps you win. It's important in winning, so we work hard at it."

For instance, he has established a program that helps the players explore investment opportunities so that when they leave the game of football they are prepared to face the real world. The Packers also have a family programs director who helps players and their families adjust to living in Green Bay.

Because the African-American population in the city is around only 1 percent, Green Bay has not been a particularly attractive spot for minorities. Since the bulk of the team is made up of African-American players, Holmgren has done a few things to help the situation, such as having the team cater food from a well-liked Milwaukee restaurant for the players. It's a little thing, but one the players seem to appreciate. It's also something no other coach has ever tried in Green Bay.

As an assistant with the 49ers, Holmgren was in a much different role than he is in now, and it revealed to him the importance of understanding the modern-day player. The 49ers of the mid-1980's were a very talented team, but they also had a lot of different personalties in the locker room. A personable fellow by nature, Holmgren became very close to his players — too close, in fact, for a head coach. But he had the luxury of being an assistant, and he learned a lot about the players' side of things.

"He was very down to earth," 49ers tight end Brent Jones recalls. "You liked to go out and play hard for him. He had a close relationship with a lot of guys, maybe to the point of it being a detriment. He got real close to guys. He was very emotional. He really liked the players."

In the world of day-to-day operations, Holmgren immediately urged the Packers to build a bigger practice facility so that potential free agents wouldn't be scared off by the cold weather in Green Bay. Even today, he moves the team inside as soon as temperatures dip into the high 40's because he wants his team focusing on the mental aspects of practice and not on how cold their hands and feet are.

In addition, he is very cognizant about not overworking his players. Having played the game, he understands how long the season is and what a toll it takes on the body. Toward the latter half of the season he limits full-pads practices to no more than once a week.

"He's a coach that I guarantee to a man that the Packers like playing for," said San Francisco 49ers quarterback Steve Young, who played for Holm-gren at B.Y.U. and with the 49ers. "They love the idea he's willing to be accountable for all the actions that he has. He's also a great motivator. And I think he's superior in his football gamesmanship."

Holmgren demands excellence from all of his players, but one of the things he won't do is rip them publicly. In fact, there are times he has accepted blame for the team's failures, such as when the Packers lost on the road at Detroit in 1995 to go 5-3 at the halfway point.

"I was so disappointed, I don't know if I've felt

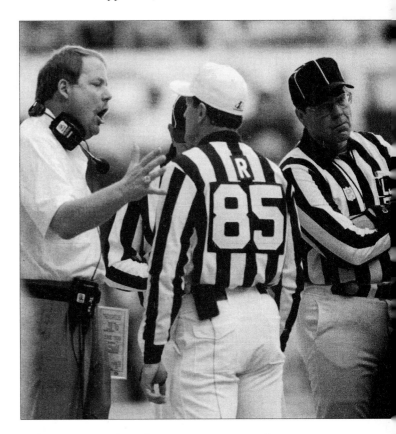

Holmgren expresses his views on a penalty.

In the final seconds against Atlanta in the 1995 playoffs, Holmgren is doused with water by his players.

After the drenching, Edgar Bennett shares a towel — and a laugh — with Holmgren.

like that in a long time," Holmgren said after the loss. "But I've got to blame myself if we lose to a team that I think we should beat. I can't always be pointing fingers at the other people. Instead of just going right down the line and ripping, all I said (to the players) was, 'This was mine.' "

Of course, part of Holmgren's winning philosophy isn't so player-friendly. The demands he puts on every individual in the locker room, particularly his quarterback, are enough to bring a man to his knees.

More than anything, Holmgren can't tolerate mental mistakes. Practices are not particularly long in Green Bay, with the longest going a little less than two hours on Thursdays. So Holmgren expects them to be run flawlessly, with attention to fundamentals being paramount.

In many ways, he's like a high school teacher who's bent on making sure his students get a college scholarship. He doesn't intend to tell his players anything twice, because if they can't get it the first time they probably aren't qualified to be in his classroom.

"I'm a teacher," says Holmgren, who earned a bachelor of science degree at Southern California and taught history at two San Francisco-area high schools. "In the development of young people, you realize communicating is different. But, what you find is, when dealing with older athletes — very gifted, very skilled athletes — the transfer of knowledge doesn't change all that much. They're like big little kids."

Both wide receiver Robert Brooks and running back Edgar Bennett learned Holmgren's intolerance for mistakes during their rookie seasons. Brooks kept dropping balls and jumping offsides, and Holmgren sat him down after a particularly bad performance against the New York Giants in 1992. Bennett, meanwhile, fumbled during a critical series against the Lions on Nov. 1 and was benched for three games.

Both players, who are now two of Holmgren's most reliable offensive weapons, took the message to heart. Bennett, in particular, turned the experience into a positive. He fumbled once more his rookie year before going 726 carries without losing a fumble.

"I got the message," Bennett said. "I wanted to play, so I wasn't going to fumble anymore."

If Holmgren expects a lot out of his backs and receivers, his demands on the quarterback are almost inhuman. Each of the quarterbacks must know the game-plan inside and out, and each is given a written test on Fridays to make sure they know formations and coverages.

Holmgren's ability to transfer his own knowledge about playing quarterback to his players is a big reason he's been so successful. The quarterback is the centerpiece of his offensive system — and when things aren't run perfectly, the offense falls apart.

He has been fortunate to coach some very talented quarterbacks in his time, starting with Marty Mornhinweg at Oak Grove High School in San Jose, Calif., and continuing with Steve Young and Robbie Bosco at B.Y.U., Joe Montana, Young and Steve Bono with the 49ers and Brett Favre in Green Bay.

There are others, too. Like Ty Detmer and Mark Brunell, who both went from backup jobs in Green Bay to starting jobs in Philadelphia and Jacksonville, respectively.

Of course, Montana, Young and Favre are the ones Holmgren is linked to most often.

"All three of those guys are very different, really,"

said Mornhinweg, who is now Holmgren's quarterbacks coach in Green Bay. "They all have different styles. The common thread between Joe, Steve and Brett is they were all coached by Mike Holmgren."

As the 1996 season progressed into something special, Holmgren's coaching talents were pressed to the limits. The Packers won some early games by big margins, and with each victory the expectation level grew both inside and outside the organization. His greatest accomplishment was convincing the players that each game was critical even if it was against Tampa Bay or St. Louis.

Players such as wide receiver Don Beebe, who played for all four of Buffalo's Super Bowl teams, noticed halfway through the season that the focus was centered on winning games and not on the Super Bowl itself.

"We were pretty good year-to-year," Beebe said of the Bills. "I think there were plateaus, but we were always striving to get better like this team does. I think it's more so even here because Mike stresses it more than Marv (Levy) did.

"He's never satisfied with what we've accomplished. 'We're 8-1. Big deal. So what if you're 8-1, and if you finish 8-8, then 8-1 is nothing.' I think that's what Mike really stresses."

It is clear that Holmgren has a definite plan for winning, much like the one that Walsh had for the 49ers. But he is his own man and his ability to relate to people has probably taken him farther than any power sweep or three wide-receiver set ever could.

A winner at every level, Holmgren has helped the Packers dig themselves out of a deep depression, one that has lasted the better part of 30 years.

"That's the first thing I said: 'This guy really wants to win bad,'" said free safety Eugene Robinson, who joined the team before the '96 season via a trade. "And he's trying to communicate that to everybody on this team."

CHAPTER SIX

A Gunslinger with Swagger

By Thomas George

The New York Times

He walked into the news conference with a bright smile, that signature stubble on his face, eager to share his thoughts. This was a special day for Brett Favre, the swashbuckling quarterback with the rifle arm and the fancy footwork. He was meeting with reporters to talk about his latest accomplishment.

No, this was not on Monday, when Favre was named the National Football League's most valuable player for his sparkling season. No, this was four years ago when Favre had been traded, after one season in Atlanta, from the Falcons to the Green Bay Packers. And no, it was not for any drama he had created on the field. It was to announce that Favre had been selected as the Wisconsin spokesman for the annual Punt, Pass and Kick competition.

"I grew up in the organization, so it was a natural thing for me to do," Favre said, recalling that day. "We bring all of the kids in for halftime of one of our games during the season to compete and I always go and talk to them before the game. It's something I still do."

No surprise there. With all of the hoopla surrounding him now, Brett Favre still makes time to finish the little things he starts.

At the time, Don Majkowski was the quarterback, the magic in Green Bay, and Favre was a backup. Turn the page four seasons later and we find Majkowski a backup with the Detroit Lions and

Favre the darling of the 1995 season. He was named the league's m.v.p. because he threw 38 touchdown passes and led the Packers to an 11-5 record and their first division crown in 23 years. He won it because he threw 33 touchdown passes and only 3 interceptions in 11 Packer victories and 5 touchdown passes and 10 interceptions in five losses.

He won it in part because the Packers are 37-24 with him as the starter. He won it because the Packers finished first in the league in scoring inside the opposition's 20-yard line and in third-down conversions.

And maybe he won it because he expected to win it. That is the thing about Brett Favre — stubborn, confident, excitable and a pro's pro at the ripe age of 26. The thing that separates him from other players is that he is all about finishing what he starts.

This is great news for Packers fans. One playoff game (the 37-20 victory over Atlanta here last Sunday) is complete and another huge one awaits at San Francisco against the 49ers on Saturday.

When you watch Brett Favre play quarterback, you are watching the cutting edge of the position in pro football in the 1990's. Today's pro quarterbacks must have a strong arm. They must be mobile. They must make quick and proper reads. They must feature a rocket release.

Brett Favre owns each of those traits and more.

"The ability to improvise is the most important thing," Favre said. "You can practice something all week and rarely when you get into a game does it go exactly like you practiced it. Over my four years I've

Brett Favre threw 38 TD's while leading the Packers to an 11-5 regular-season record in 1995.

been able to make plays. Everybody in this league can catch, block, tackle, run, whatever their strength may be. Fewer can do the things they are not asked to do. I think that's my knack — making something happen when nothing is there."

His game against the Falcons illustrated that. On one pass play Favre looked right, looked over the middle, looked right and then whirled and threw the ball nearly 20 yards downfield to the left to receiver Antonio Freeman. It looked as if Freeman was the fifth option on the play. Favre found him.

He walks the tightrope, a fine line, indeed, and comes so close to crossing it in overconfidence and selfishness. But Favre's high self-esteem is one of his strongest assets.

In an interview recently, he said, essentially, that he was the glue for the Packers and if he played well they won and if he did not they lost. Turns out, he was right. But it sounded so nasty, so self-serving. That is why Packers coach Mike Holmgren had a chat with Favre about that and now asks a member of the Packers public-relations staff to be present for any of Favre's one-on-one interviews.

Favre needing a baby sitter? This gunslinger who shoots from the lip as easily as he does from the pocket? Sounds comical. Holmgren wants to know what was said via his own source if controversy arises again. Favre shrugs it off and rolls right along, not worrying about stepping on any toes.

"I did expect success to come," he said matter-of-factly today before the Packers' practice. "I've always expected great things of myself.

"It comes from my parents. It comes from the environment I grew up in in a small town, Kiln, in Mississippi. Things never came easy for us, but I always had a feeling things would work out. Maybe the only time in football that I questioned myself was when Atlanta traded me. They never gave me a chance there. It hurt. But then I found out I had

been traded for a No. 1 draft pick and that the Packers had big plans for me. I got over that trade quickly.

"Mike Holmgren has been good for me and so have the Packers but I don't think it mattered when it came to success. I wasn't one of those guys that wasn't going to play pro ball here or there. I would play anywhere anyone wanted me. I could have played in the run and shoot in Atlanta or for any coach in any offense. But this offense does allow me to put up good numbers."

Favre is fortunate. He could have wound up with a struggling offense and scheme like the New Orleans Saints, or even in Detroit where, at the time he entered the league from Southern Mississippi, he could have become part of the circus of quarterbacks (Rodney Peete, Andre Ware and Erik Kramer) that the Lions featured.

No, he was tabbed by Holmgren to start early after joining the team from Atlanta and he had Holmgren, one of the best quarterback tutors and offensive tacticians around.

Favre is fortunate. And dependable.

"We are perfect for each other," said the Packers' star receiver, Robert Brooks, who emerged this season along with Favre. "I'm not sure it was by design. The fact that he can break down a defense with his movement and his mind and get the ball into tight coverage or lob it in the end zone is the key. When you are running routes on the backside and you are not the primary receiver, it makes you run them harder. You are potentially never out of the play with Brett."

Since Holmgren comes from the 49ers and since the Packers run the 49ers' offense — "identical," Favre said — the Green Bay versus San Francisco matchup should be intriguing. How will the 49ers and defensive coordinator Pete Carroll choose to defend Favre? Few teams have devised a formula that works.

After completing a pass, Favre receives a friendly jolt from Dallas' Charles Haley in 1994.

"Steve Young and I are going to be going at each other," Favre said.

"It's the old versus the young. I've watched a lot of film on Steve to see how he runs this offense. They have the No. 1 defense in the league. It will be fun to see how we stack up against them."

It will be fun, particularly, to see how Favre stacks up against the defending Super Bowl champions. So much fun to see if he can, again, finish what he starts.

CHAPTER SEVEN

"Reggie Lives the Life He Preaches"

By Dave Anderson

The New York Times

Hardly a day passes without a name athlete on the sports blotter. Illegal drugs. Guns. sexual assault. Spousal abuse. Alcohol abuse. Driving under the influence.

Most athletes, like most people, are solid citizens, but by the nature of what constitutes news, the rotten apples' names are in the headlines, their faces on television. More often than not, it seems, the rotten apples are the familiar names.

And then there's Reggie White.

He's not just the Green Bay Packers' defensive end, he's an ordained minister. He's not just the National Football League's career sack leader, he's the voice behind a campaign that could contribute as much as $8 million from N.F.L. players to help rebuild America's burned black churches.

"It just shows," he has said of the burned churches, "we've got problems we don't want to believe we have."

One of the burned churches is his church, the Inner City Community Church in Knoxville, Tenn., where he is the associate pastor, where he preached occasionally before flames lighted up the snowy darkness there Jan. 8.

"I believe that out of every bad situation, something great will happen," he has said. "When my church burned, it showed me that God is calling me to have an impact, to rally people from different ethnic backgrounds."

Of the $1.2 million required to rebuild his church, about $230,000 has been raised, mostly from predominantly white Packer fans in Wisconsin.

"Reggie lives the life he preaches about," said the Rev. David Upton, the Inner City pastor. "He's always reached out to help other people."

Now 34, White preached in high school in Chattanooga and at the University of Tennessee, where he was an all-American. In his years with the Eagles, he preached on Philadelphia street corners to teen-agers: stay in school, stay off drugs.

With a four-year, $19 million contract, the 6-foot-5-inch, 300-pound All-Pro has put his money where his mouth is. Two years ago, he helped organize the Community Development Bank in Knoxville for those who couldn't qualify for loans.

"To get it going," Upton said, "Reggie put up $1 million of his own."

Over the last 18 months, the despicable burning of some three dozen black churches, primarily in the South, has created the largest Federal arson investigation in the nation's history: nearly 250 Federal Bureau of Investigation agents along with another 250 state troopers and local police, some $21.5 million in additional funding.

And now pro football's Minister of Defense has

Reggie White wraps up Raiders quarterback Jeff Hostetler in 1994.

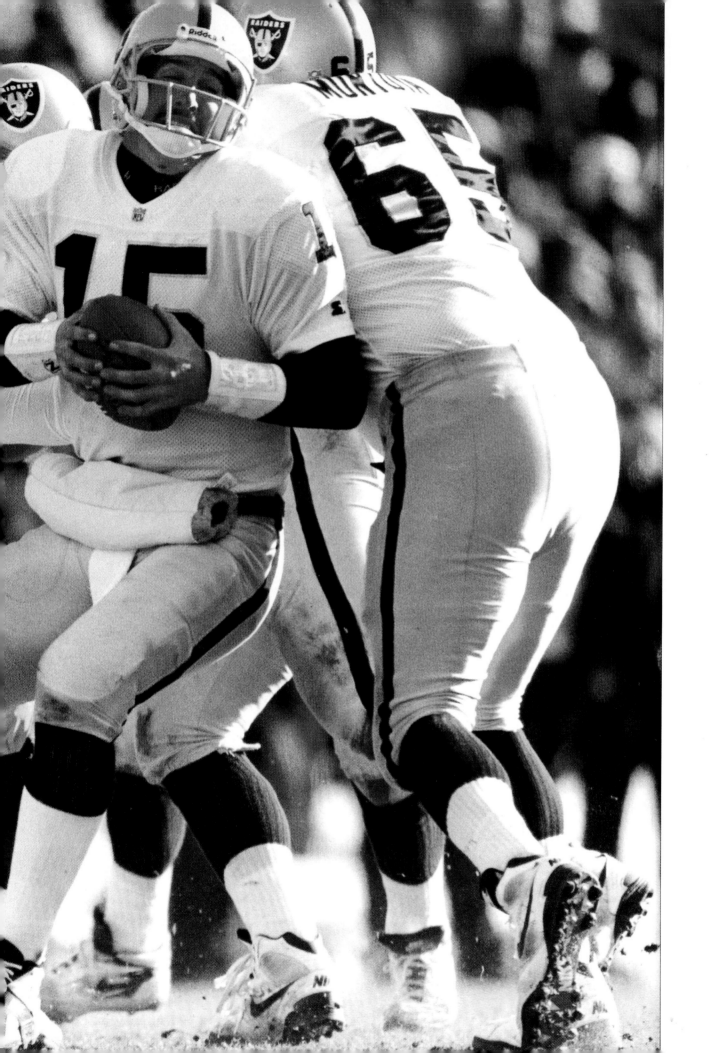

challenged N.F.L. players to join the cause.

"Reggie mentioned this idea to me before his church was burned," said Gene Upshaw, the executive director of the N.F.L. Players Association. "He remembered how we did the same thing for the United Negro College Fund a few years ago. The players would sign over their $5,000 rebate checks from the union."

Each union member's annual dues are $5,000, but if licensing revenue pays the union's costs, all or part of that $5,000 is returned.

"I'll talk about it to the players, we'll send out letters, the player rep on each team will discuss it," Upshaw said. "The potential is $8 million for a foundation that would administer the money. This problem of churches being burned is not going away."

Upshaw remembered his Baptist church in Robstown, Tex., a few hours from the Mexican border.

"It was the glue to the community," he said. "Every Sunday you went to church all day. You had Sunday school at 9 in the morning, a worship and a sermon at 11, a service at 2 in the afternoon, another service at 6, then a worship and sometimes another sermon at 7:30. And if you weren't there, everybody knew it."

And when churches burn, everybody knows it.

"People always ask me," Reggie White has said, " 'As a minister, how do you justify the violence in football?' But I tell them: 'Football's not a violent game, football is an aggressive game. Violence is people shooting other people in the street.' "

Or people burning other people's churches.

White waves to loyal Packers fans after a victory.

CHAPTER EIGHT

A New Dynasty in Titletown

By Michael Bauman

After wandering in the post-Lombardi era wildnerness for nearly a quarter century, the Green Bay Packers are headed toward the football promised land. Or at least they can see it from here.

How did this happen? How did all those years of futility very rapidly turn to success? How did resignation turn to hope? How did five winning seasons in 24 years suddenly become a steady march back to the top of the National Football League?

Here's as good an answer as any: The Packers stopped struggling and started winning when they stopped trying to find the next coaching personification of Vince Lombardi. They started the long road back, from oblivion to the Super Bowl, from defeat to dynasty-in-the-making, when they hired Michael George Holmgren as coach.

"The best thing I did was get Mike Holmgren in here," says Packers general manager Ron Wolf, who hired Holmgren. "The second best thing was Brett Favre."

When you consider that Favre was the 1995 N.F.L. most valuable player, that's about as large a recommendation as the general manager could make. And it is not an overstatement.

A bit of Green-and-Gold history might put Holmgren's success in a perspective that is both glowing and proper. The Packers have known both feast and famine in large measures. For all the glory attached to the franchise, there have been only three coaches in its history with winning records — Curly

Lambeau Field, capacity 60,790, provides the Packers with a college-like setting.

Lambeau, Lombardi and now Holmgren.

Being the coach of the Green Bay Packers is the best job in Wisconsin — if you're winning. This is the smallest city in major professional sports. The Packers are not merely in the spotlight; they *are* the spotlight. Second-guessing the coach is not merely a pastime, but a civic duty. If a coach loses here, the losses will follow him to the supermarket, to the service station, up the driveway and practically into the house.

The response to Holmgren has obviously not been the same as the response to Lombardi, who became, in these parts, as much a deity as a coach. Holmgren is much more mortal, much more accessible. But the affection for Holmgren and for his team is legitimate.

Lambeau Field has grown to a capacity of more

than 60,000. If the weather gets bad — no, when the weather gets bad — the no-show total might climb all the way above 100. The waiting list time for season tickets can be measured in light years. Retailers throughout the state report that sales rise after Packers victories and fall after Packers defeats. The fan following has not faltered in Green Bay. It was there in the long years of defeat, but now it has a reason larger than patience for being in attendance.

In fact, the "Titletown, U.S.A." monicker of the Lombardi years is more appropriate than ever. Thousands of Packers fans now follow the team to road games. It does not matter where; Chicago, Tampa, Minneapolis, Seattle. They pay scalpers' prices to attend, but they sometimes outnumber the hometown rooters. If there is any question, you can tell the Green Bay fans: They'll be the ones wearing the cheeseheads. There weren't any of those in the Lombardi era, possibly because Vince wouldn't have allowed that kind of headgear in a football stadium.

These current Packers are five N.F.L. championships short of the Lombardi era dynasty. but they are not short on affection. No other team and its following make such a direct connection. Packers who score touchdowns have taken to leaping into the Lambeau Field stands in celebration. It's sort of a returned favor for all the loyalty and devotion.

There is, once again, something of a religious fervor attached to following the Packers. Even if the Packers weren't so successful, you could get some of that listening to Reggie White. He's the premier defensive end of this era, or perhaps any era, but he's also "the minister of defense," because he is an ordained Baptist minister. White sees football as one more way to testify to his faith.

After two of his sacks had preserved a victory over Denver, the entire Lambeau Field crowd chanted his name. When White was asked what it felt like, hearing that adoration, he responded: "Praise God."

George Teague fires up the crowd after a TD.

Then there's Favre, whose scrambling, gambling, give-up-your-body-for-the-cause style has endeared him to Green Bay fans. He may be a long way from his home in Kiln, Miss., but it may be that a small town in southern Mississippi is not so vastly different from a small city in northeastern Wisconsin. Favre is like an adopted son in Green Bay. His indiscretions are forgiven and his courage is admired.

But the one Green-and-Gold figure that ties all of this together for the public is the coach. Holmgren is perfect for the role and not only because he wins. He seems to be everywhere in Wisconsin; on his own television show, appearing regularly on radio progams throughout the state, and selling Buicks in commer-

Robert Brooks enjoys one of his famous TD jumps into the stands.

Craig Newsome (21) is welcomed by his teammates onto the field during the pre-game announcement of the team's starters.

cials. But nobody complains that he is over-exposed.

For this job, he is out of central casting. Big man. Scandanavian. Understated in public. Known to be compassionate. Also gruff when the situation demands that. He is a Californian, but he could be the guy next door anywhere in Wisconsin.

The team also happily reflects the population. The Packers are not in ego-overload. There are stars, certainly, but they seem like human beings. And they don't play soft. All of it adds up to a flood of community affection. An autograph-signing at a shopping center can draw thousands of spectators. These people understand that they cannot all get autographs. But they can all get to see a Packer, in the

flesh, and that seems to be enough.

People here take great joy in not only the Packers' victories, but the Packers' anecdotes. Last December, White had a serious hamstring injury that was going to require surgery. One day after that determination was made, White had what he calls "a healing." He called the Packers' stength coach and they went to Lambeau Field where the hamstring was put through a series of tests. The hamstring had miraculously improved.

In the dark of a pre-Christmas night, as the hour approached midnight, White headed for Holmgren's house with the good news. Holmgren was just coming to the door to turn off the outside lights, when White appeared. "I thought he was Santa Claus,"

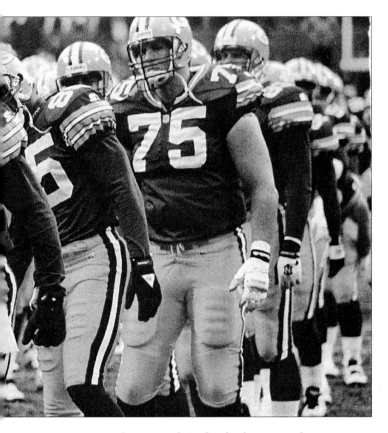

Holmgren said. And indeed, in a way, he was.

That kind of feel-good story seems to follow the Packers around these days. It is appreciated all the more because, for all those years between Lombardi and Holmgren, there wasn't much reason to feel good about the Packers. It can be a long time between dynasties. It can even be a long time between victories.

Following the glory of the Lombardi years — five N.F.L. championships in seven years, including victories in the first two Super Bowls — the Green Bay organization kept trying to somehow duplicate that feat by hiring people it thought were in the Lombardi mold.

First, there was Phil Bengston, a logical choice, since he was Lombardi's defensive coordinator. But Bengston was stuck with an aging team. The Packers went outside briefly and hired Dan Devine, but when

that didn't work wonders, either, there was even more sentiment for a return to the Lombardi era.

So the Packers hired Lombardi's brains on the field, former quarterback Bart Starr. Starr's immense popularity won for him nine seasons as Green Bay's coach. But when the former glory again was not forthcoming, the Packers hired Lombardi's brawn on the field, former tackle Forrest Gregg.

But Gregg's record was worse than Starr's record. Outside the Packers went again, this time for noted offensive coordinator Lindy Infante, who did manage a 10-6 season in 1989. But the record regressed again, and Infante's overall record was even worse than Gregg's. By autumn of 1991, the Packers were headed for a 4-12 season. Again. And there was really no hope in sight.

Throughout this era, the Packers had been both blessed and cursed by the nature of their organization. The Packers are the only major contemporary pro sports franchise that is publicly-owned. This makes them literally a community effort and explains at least in part a following that is the most loyal in sports. But it also allowed for interference in the team's operation by individuals who were not necessarily "football people."

The civilians running the Packers tried to fashion a repeat of the Lombardi era by investing all authority in a coach, just as had been done with Lombardi. Unfortunately, Lombardi could not be cloned. The Packers stumbled from coach to coach like a banana republic going through military dictators.

All of this changed in November 1991, when the president of the club, Bob Harlan, decided that was what needed here was a football man who would be general manager and who would have sole authority over the football aspects of the franchise.

Harlan chose Ron Wolf, an N.F.L. front-office veteran. Wolf's first job was to determine what would happen to Infante, who had a long-term contract. It took Wolf all of three weeks to determine that Infante was not the answer, either.

Wolf's future in Green Bay would be, he knew, determined in large part by this one decision. It appeared for a time that the choice would be Bill Parcells, who had recently won a Super Bowl with the New York Giants and then retired. But Parcells' interest in the Green Bay coaching job was of the on-again, off-again variety. Wolf moved quickly toward someone who actually seemed to want this job.

Holmgren at this time was the offensive coordinator of the San Francisco 49ers. Holmgren was being pursued by no less than six teams.

"It was a key decision and a lot of work went into it," Wolf said. "But after sitting with Mike for 15 minutes and listening to him present himself and what he liked to do on offense, it was all over."

And so, on Jan. 11, 1992 Holmgren was hired as the 11th head coach in Packers history. Wolf had to part with a second-round draft choice, since Holmgren was still under contract to the 49ers. That was, as it turned out, a tiny price to pay. The rest has been largely they all lived happily ever after.

The Packers went from 4-12 the year before Holmgren's arrival to 9-7, then 9-7 with a playoff victory; then 9-7 with another playoff victory; then 11-5 with a Central Division championship and a playoff progression all the way to the conference championship game; to the present, which means the best team Green Bay has had in 28 years and a legitimate shot at the Super Bowl.

This did not happen because the law of averages was on the Packers' side. This happened, in large part because of who Mike Holmgren was and is and the skills he brings to this task.

Publicly, Holmgren was quick to say that he was not Lombardi. This seems fairly obvious, but in the Wisconsin sports landscape, if you don't say that, someone will charge you with impersonating

Lombardi. Legends are tough to follow, even at the distance of 25 years.

But at the same time, Holmgren was equally quick to pay homage to the Green Bay football heritage. "I embrace the Green Bay tradition," Holmgren said. In fact, he is still saying that, in Seven-Up commercials.

It helped that Holmgren and Wolf just fit, like Lennon and McCartney writing lyrics and music, like Batman and Robin fighting crime, like, well, Ron and Mike rebuilding a dormant franchise.

"When Bob Harlan hired Ron Wolf and said, 'All right, you're in charge of the football operation,' then Ron hired me, that's the best situation you could be in as a coach," Holmgren says. "Ron and I talk about things and then a decision is made. Other organizations, it's not that cut and dried. For the most part there are other people involved. And the more people that are involved, in my opinion, the harder it becomes.

"I have as much responsibiliy as I want or need. The beauty of this situation is that there are no decisions made, personnel or football decisions, without the two of us talking about it. It's a great situation for a coach."

For his part, Wolf, who is brutally candid in making judgments about talent and character, fairly bursts with praise on the topic of Mike Holmgren.

"I tell you what," Wolf says, "Mike Holmgren is such a tremendous person to work with. I can't tell you how thankful I am that he's the head coach. I don't think there's a problem with egos.

"He's so upbeat. He's done a great job, part and parcel, he and his assistants, of convincing the players that they can win. Plus, he's a genuinely good, decent human being."

There is no dispute on that last point, from anyone who has had any sort of dealings with Holmgren. It is the kind of thing that is sensed by Wisconsin people, who want the Packers coach to be successful, but also want him to be a good guy.

Yes, Holmgren is candid and open, bright and diligent. You could say that, on the basis of what kind of individual he is, he deserves all the success he has had. And yet, contemporary pro sports can eat up nice guys. Being a good guy still counts, but there is more to the story than that.

Holmgren and Wolf had to dramatically improve the caliber of players on their roster. And to do that, in the new era of free agency, they had to be salesmen. They had to sell the Green Bay franchise to players. Before they arrived on the scene that would have been like selling a Ford Pinto. Coaches throughout the league used to threaten misbehaving players with trades to Green Bay. It was an outpost. It was an Artic exile. It was not a favored destination among the N.F.L.'s upwardly mobile.

The breakthrough sales job was accomplished after the 1992 season. Reggie White was the king of free agents. If you could get Reggie White, you could get anybody. Naturally, nobody gave the Packers a chance.

White said then and says now that God told him to go to Green Bay. Some people chuckle at that, but to White it meant that he had to be at peace with whatever decision he made. He is a deeply and sincerely religious man, and to him this was foremost. But he also says that he was very much impressed with Holmgren and Wolf.

They did not roll out the red carpet with Reggie White. They did not wine and dine him. They talked about the Green Bay football legacy and what a great place this was for football. Apparently, both heaven and earth were moved.

After White's signing, the free-agent dam burst. The Green Bay roster is now dotted with valuable free agents, such as Sean Jones at the other defensive end, or Santana Dotson at defensive tackle. Not that long ago, players of this stature would have considered

Sterling Sharpe was Brett Favre's favorite receiver until an injury forced his retirement.

Green Bay as a punishment, not as a home. But with Mike Holmgren as coach, it's a different matter.

"The credit for that goes directly to Mike Holmgren and his staff," Wolf says. "They have done a magnificent job of changing an attitude and a perception here of what the Packers are all about. Not only on the field, but off the field as well.

"People throughout the league no longer look at Green Bay as 'The Frozen Tundra.' They look at it as a great place to come and play professional football.

"There's a certain air of cockiness now among the people in our organization. We are confident we have the best to offer any player in the National Football League."

People in Wisconsin love that *frozen tundra* stuff. The Packers, in their first four seasons under Holmgren, were 11-5 overall in December, but were unbeaten in December games at Lambeau Field. This is seen as the way things should be in Wisconsin winter: The wind howls. The snow flies. The Packers win at home, where the elements are their brothers.

Holmgren says "I suffer more than anybody in cold weather." This kind of statement just endears him more to the local populace. The poor guy is from California, and he's shivering out there on the sideline, but the team is still winning.

A more directly significant piece of work by Holmgren has been the development of Favre, from a strong-armed but erratic athlete into one of the most accomplished quarterbacks in the game. This did not happen quickly or easily. In 1993, his second season as starting quarterback, Favre threw 24 interceptions, and there were concerns in Packerland that the he would never get beyond the stage of young gun.

Holmgren encouraged and coaxed and supported the young quarterback, but he also drove him relentlessly. As time wore on, there was less coaxing and more driving until ...

"In 1994, we lost a game to Philadelphia and I didn't help Brett or wasn't able to help him one bit that game," Holmgren says. "That had never happened before. That's when I realized things had to change."

It may not be coincidental that Favre's emergence into a top-flight quarterback dates almost directly from that time. And when Favre's addiction to the painkiller Vicodin became public in the spring of 1996, it was Holmgren who not only stood by Favre's side at the public announcement of the problem, but rallied his players in support of Favre.

"He just let us know that we were going to handle it like a family," wide receiver Robert Brooks says. "Anything that happens within a family, you pull closer and work it out."

Again, that is just how it went. Brooks also says that Holmgren is "like your father." By that he means that Holmgren has the ability to show players that he cares about them, not only as units of weight and strength and speed, but as human beings. And at the other end of the dad spectrum, he has the ability to get very, very upset with his surrogate sons.

It's a happy ship in Green Bay now. Contemporary football can be a minefield for coaches, with agents, free agency, player ego trips and vastly increased media attention all providing the possibility of potential explosions. Not here.

"The chemistry on this team is as good as any I've ever been around," Reggie White says. "Everybody kids each other, and the ego thing is low."

When the Packers are winning, the chemistry around the entire State of Wisconsin is also very good. The dynasty of the Lombardi era may never be completely repeated. But with Mike Holmgren and the current Packers, there is direction and victory and legitimate hope. Green Bay, nearing "Titletown" status again, is, at the very least, "Footballtown, U.S.A."

CHAPTER NINE

The Leader of the Pack

By Pete Dougherty

On a hot July afternoon this past summer, Mike Holmgren sat in a school desk just inside the entrance to the Green Bay Packers' Oneida Street practice field.

Outside the fenced-in field, a couple hundred Packers fans waited patiently for their turn to step inside the gate and get an autograph from the Packers' head coach.

They were among the 1,000-plus people who watch the Packers practice nearly every day in training camp, and many of them stay around after the workouts to get autographs from players. Whether they knew it or not, Holmgren was giving them a special treat, because training camp is one of the busiest times of the year for N.F.L. coaches. They have to plan and conduct two practices a day, study practice film each night, and meet regularly with their assistant coaches trying daily to determine what's working well and what isn't on their offense and defense, and who should make their team and who shouldn't.

On three separate afternoons during training camp this past summer, Holmgren sat at that desk for 45 minutes to an hour, signing autographs for whomever happened to be there. It's something he has done in each of his five seasons as coach, though in the first four years it was less formal. He would make the quarter-mile walk across Oneida Street and the Lambeau Field parking lot to the Packers' offices, surrounded by a mob and signing autographs as he went. He stopped doing that at the urging of the Packers' security staff because of safety concerns. Setting up the desk was his idea.

Taking that time to indulge Packers fans certainly isn't the biggest reason Holmgren has become such a fan favorite in Wisconsin. But it illustrates the bond he has solidified with Packers fans and the respect he shows everyone, whether it be fans, media, the Packers' equipment men or players. As he seems to do with nearly everyone outside the Packers organization, Holmgren during his autograph sessions displays unusual patience at a time when the pressures of his job and constraints on his time are the greatest.

"There's a warmth there that people recognize when they see him," says Bob Harlan, the Packers' team president.

Of course, the main reason Holmgren has become so popular in Wisconsin in his fifth season as the Packers' head coach is much simpler: He wins.

Packers fans, after all, have been starved for a winner for nearly 30 years. Ever since Vince Lombardi bolted Green Bay for the Washington Redskins after Super Bowl II, each succeeding coach has left the Packers with a record below .500 and a worse winning percentage than the man before him. That's five straight coaches: Phil Bengston (.476 winning percentage) Dan Devine (.472), Bart Starr (.408), Forrest Gregg (.403) and Lindy Infante (.375).

Until Holmgren. Through the 9th game of the 1996 season, his 4-year record with the Packers was 50-30, and during that time they accomplished a

Robert Brooks attempts to escape a Chicago tackler.

handful of feats that this franchise hadn't attained for more than two decades. In 1993, Holmgren's second season, they won a playoff game for the first time since 1967, which was Lombardi's last year. In '94

they went to the playoffs in back-to-back seasons for the first time since 1966 and '67.

In '95 they won the N.F.C. Central Division title for the first time since 1972, and then went on to the N.F.C. Championship game for the first time since the historic 'Ice Bowl' win over the Cowboys on New Year's Eve in '67.

By the midway point of 1996, the Packers were the most dominating team in the N.F.L., and for the first time since Lombardi, talk of a Super Bowl in Green Bay was more than just overly optimistic chatter from zealous Packers fans.

"Now people are looking at Holmgren basically in the same way as Lombardi," said Pat Riemer, a Green Bay-area native and bartender at a long-time hangout for Packers fans in downtown Green Bay, The Candlestick Lounge. "That's kind of scary. But you look at everything he's done for this team in the last five years, after 25 years of losing, people love what he's done. When's the last time people have been able to talk about the Super Bowl and actually have a shot at it?"

There's no underselling what winning means to a coach's popularity anywhere, and Green Bay is no different. There's no better illustration than back in 1989, during Infante's one winning season, when the Packers finished 10-6 and a tie-breaker away from making the playoffs. Near the end of that year, a local TV station conducted a call-in poll asking who was the best coach in Packers' history. Infante beat out Lombardi.

"Winning is the key, no doubt about it," Harlan said. "But there's another factor as well."

And that gets back to Holmgren's general patience with people, which he has shown so consistently over the past 4 years that it can't be dismissed as simply a public-relations act.

For instance, before the weekly taping of his TV show, he takes the time to chat with the audience for several minutes to get warmed up for the show, mixing humor with football talk. When the segment for fans' questions comes up, he listens patiently, then answers in a friendly, professorial manner that is in sharp contrast, for instance, to his predecessor, Infante, who often was curt and defensive to fans' questions on his TV show.

He displays that patience on a regular basis in training camp, when almost daily the Packers have one business group or another as guests on the sideline for their morning practice. After a short post-practice press conference with the media, Holmgren always addresses the visitors for a few minutes, mixing humor with information and indulging the group by answering a couple questions. Sometimes in those talks he's asked a naively brutal question that he never would get from even a hardened media, yet he never belittles the question or questioner.

"I don't think it's something he endures," said Gary Reynolds, an assistant coach with the Packers who doubles as Holmgren's administrative assistant. "I do think he has a healthy respect for fans and their support for the the team and for him in particular. I think he feels it's important."

Holmgren also has endeared himself to the common man with some of his activities away from the football field. He rides a Harley-Davidson motorcycle, which he takes on the quarter-mile trip to and from practice, weather permitting, and uses in occasional rides for charity. It has helped foster a folk-hero image similar to former Marquette basketball coach Al McGuire and current Chicago Bulls coach Phil Jackson, who also ride motorcycles. In the coaching business, many head men at least appear to be one-dimensional and all business and discipline, but the motorcycle has helped give all three of those men a more radical, down-to-earth persona in the public eye.

Mark Chmura gathers in a key pass against San Diego.

"He's not a snobbish coach," said Mark Pyatt, a lifelong Packers fan who lives in Green Bay. "You think everybody (coaches professionally) for the prestige. With him, it seems like he's there just to do

The pride of the Packers: a gang-tackling defense.

it. It sure seems like it, anyway."

This is not to suggest that Holmgren is in any way soft or too nice a guy. You don't win as many games as he has without having a hard side. Despite his avuncular manner off the field and general stoic demeanor on the sidelines during games, he regular flashes his temper and intolerence for mistakes on the practice field and off.

He is demanding of his players, and even more demanding of his assistant coaches.

"He can buckle it up when he has to," Reynolds said. "He gets on assistant coaches, real hard, I've

coached in. He later was a head coach in high school, then went on as an assistant coach with San Francisco State and B.Y.U., and then the San Francisco 49ers before coming to Green Bay.

"I think he has more patience than most people," Reynolds said. "He's probably always been that way. He probably hasn't changed as he's risen in his station. He's probably the same Mike Holmgren who was a high school teacher."

That might help explain why Holmgren has been successful in the first place. In a new era of professional football, where players in free agency can choose where they will play, he has been instrumental in luring a star such as Reggie White to Green Bay, a place that had become known among many players as a Siberia in the N.F.L. He also defused a potentially divisive holdout on the eve of the regular-season opener in 1994, when All-Pro receiver Sterling Sharpe skipped the Packers' Saturday walk-through practice because of a contractual squabble but returned to the team that night after a meeting with Holmgren.

With the big player turnover each year that has accompanied free agency, teams change significantly in most seasons, and the coach has to bring a new group together every year. It takes more than browbeating to do that.

"He's just a real person," said Ray Nitschke, the Hall of Fame linebacker who played on five Packers championship teams in the 1960's. "He enjoys himself and has fun with things. You like to see him enjoy himself, he's his own man. He's certainly a coach of the 90's."

It's a far different game in dealing with players than in the 60's, when the volcanic Lombardi ruled the N.F.L. and became a legend in Wisconsin. But Nitschke, who lives in Green Bay and talks to Holmgren several times a year, sees an important similarity between the two.

seen him do it plenty of times. But never never when it's not called for."

Nevertheless, Holmgren's consistently earthy manner off the field has helped endear him to Wisconsinites. Perhaps it stems in part from the route he took to the N.F.L. He began his coaching career as an assistant coach in high school in the San Francisco area, and said he lost the first 22 games he

"(Holmgren) treats everybody as if they're special," he said. "He's tremendous that way. Lombardi did the same thing. You're only as good as the people around you. He cares about his people, and Lombardi cared about his, too."

Holmgren also has been successful with the media, both locally and nationally.

During the football season, he generally conducts three press conferences each week in the Packers' media auditorium — on Mondays to recap the most recent game, then again on Wednesdays and again on Sunday right after the game. He also holds a short impromptu press conference on the field after practice on Fridays.

He almost always greets one or two reporters personally each time, and he rarely shows impatience or irritation to any question, whether it comes from the reporters who regularly cover the team or someone covering his or her first practice.

That's in stark contrast to some of the previous coaches in Green Bay. Starr, for instance, regularly had run-ins with reporters, and his hypersensitivity to criticism generally is regarded a big reason he never succeeded as a head coach. Infante came across superbly on television because he was quick with a quip, but he often displayed a sour side when the cameras weren't on and had a running feud with one local reporter who especially got under his skin.

Holmgren has become upset with local reporters and has confronted them on several occasions. But he always conducts those meetings one-on-one and never has responded with personal attacks or held a grudge. That certainly has helped him avoid problems within his team, because he hasn't become so consumed by a media-related problem that it affected his performance in the rest of his job, and it surely has helped his public image at large, because much of his public persona is relayed through a reporters' lens.

"He's better (with the media) than a lot I've seen

come through here," said Harlan, who has been with the Packers' front office since 1971. "He's blunt and honest about things and will tell the good with the bad."

But mainly, Holmgren has endeared himself because he has made it fun again for the fans in Green Bay. They like their coach, they're entertained by his team, and they are enjoying every second of being back among the N.F.L.'s elite for the first time in 30 years.

They liked the way last season how he shared the

Following a victory, Reggie White receives congratulations from Packers' fans.

Packers' first home playoff win since '67, when he circled Lambeau Field and shook hands with the front-row fans after the Packers' win over Atlanta. And they paid him back this season, when the Packers gave up 17 straight points in the first half of a Monday night game against San Francisco and left the field at halftime trailing, 17-6. At a time when the Packers expected to get booed, the fans gave them a cheer of encouragement instead, and they eventually went home happy when Chris Jacke kicked a game-winning 52-yard field goal in overtime.

"You look at the way this offense is set up and has played this year, it's so fun to watch," said Reimer, the bartender. "They've won a lot of blowouts. Fans appreciate that. They know nine out of 10 times they're not going to a losing game, and they know it's going to be fun to watch."

CHAPTER TEN

The Difference was Holmgren

By Bud Lea

On the evening of Dec. 21, 1991, Green Bay was gushing, with rumors. Earlier that day, the Packers had played their best game of the season and had routed the Minnesota Vikings, 27-7, in the Metrodome. It was a game that made it so easy to forget how disinterested and poorly the team had played most of the year.

Ron Wolf, the team's first real general manager with full power to hire and fire, had made up his mind on the Packers' short flight home. There was something terribly wrong here, either in attitude or ability. Coach Lindy Infante, with three years remaining on his contract, and all 10 assistants would be fired.

Wolf and team president Bob Harlan drove to the Packers' complex at Lambeau Field after the chartered plane had landed. The decision was pretty cut and dried.

"We sat there for an hour, and he gave me his reasons," Harlan said. "He told me he wanted to do it, and why he wanted to do it, and who he wanted to go after. I said, 'Fine, let's do it.' "

In four seasons at Green Bay, Infante had a 24-40 record. Anywhere else, Infante's departure would have been a foregone conclusion.

But this was Green Bay, where Bart Starr managed to hang around for nine seasons, solely on the promise of better tomorrows.

As Wolf told Infante, 4-12 was not acceptable. A 4-12 record didn't reflect well on this once-proud franchise, and it could not be ignored.

This entire operation had been run so masterly by Vince Lombardi that the Packers' ruling seven-man Executive Committee thought for years that another person could do it in the dual role of head coach and general manager. Just find that man, and the Pack would be back.

Instead, what followed was a steady downward path from Lombardi's .757 winning percentage to Phil Bengtson's .488 to Dan Devine's .473 to Bart Starr's .409 to Forrest Gregg's .404 to Lindy Infante's .375.

"It was like walking down a ladder," Harlan said. "Because Lombardi could do it, we thought everyone could do it. That was our biggest mistake. As the game grew and became more complexed, we finally decided it could not be done that way any longer."

Now that the Packers had fired Infante and were officially out of scapegoats, Wolf, 24 days on the job as the newly appointed general manager, sat on the hot seat. Before too long, Packer fans would find out what kind of football man Ron Wolf was and if the best was yet to come.

Wolf had scheduled interviews with former Seattle Seahawks coach Chuck Knox and Terry Robiskie, the offensive coordinator of the then- Los

Dan Devine had a 25-28-4 record during 1971-74.

Angeles Raiders. The man Wolf wanted was Bill Parcells, the former coach of the New York Giants and winner of two Super Bowls.

There were tremendous parallels between Lombardi and Parcells. Both of them said their lives, along with their coaching philosophies, were shaped when they were assistant coaches at the U.S. Military Academy. Both had coached with the New York Giants. Lombardi won an N.F.L. championship in his third season at Green Bay. Parcells won it in his fourth at New York.

Parcells, who was working for NBC, had recently undergone a coronary angioplasty. When he told Wolf he wasn't interested in the Green Bay job, Wolf turned his attention elsewhere.

Wolf was nearing his 30th year in pro football, and his calling card was knowing talent. He had dealt exclusively with scouting and drafting players. Never had he been in a position to make a decision of this magnitude, one that would affect the Packers for years to come.

Somewhere, there was an up-and-coming, hungry guy who may be a perfect fit for the Packers. Wolf found his man in San Francisco, and the faithful along the banks of the Fox became nervous.

Mike Holmgren as the Packers' coach? The 43-year-old man who had been coaching as an assistant in the N.F.L. for only five years? The California guy who had never lived east of Provo, Utah?

Mike Holmgren? The 6-5, 235-pound giant who could tower over but not out-scream Forrest Gregg? The guy who was the starting quarterback at the University of Southern California and was an eighth-round draft choice of the St. Louis Cardinals in 1970, tried out with the New York Jets but was not to play in the N.F.L.?

The guy who worked for the 49ers, an organization that was not on speaking terms with the Packers? The assistant coach who had enlisted the services of one of the brassiest agents in the business, Bob LaMonte, who negotiated California quarterback Rich (The Bust) Campbell's contract with the Packers 10 years ago?

That Mike Holmgren?

Green Bay fans' jaws could not have dropped lower if Mike Ditka had campaigned for the job. The Packers had fallen into the hands of a man who had never been a head coach at any level of football.

Wolf felt enough confidence in this young offensive coordinator from the 49ers to give him almost unheard-of security and money. He also felt confident enough to return a second-round draft choice to the 49ers to allow Holmgren to get out of his contract at San Francisco.

Holmgren would leave his heart and friends and a good team in San Francisco to rescue the Roman Empire of the N.F.L.. The Packers had not won a playoff game in 11 years. Kids born in the year of the Packers' last Super Bowl appearance were 24 years old. Bart Starr was a grandpa.

On the morning of Jan. 12, 1992, the first day after he was hired, Mike Holmgren, briefcase in hand, showed up for work at his new job, and he was locked out.

The Packers had given him a five-year guaranteed contract, the use of a new Buick and their very best wishes. But they had forgotten to give him the key to the office at 1265 Lombardi Ave.

So, the first thing the new coach of the Packers did that bitter cold morning was to drive back to the Embassy Suites hotel, pick up his wife and four daughters and go house hunting. The Holmgrens planned to stay a while.

"I believe I have my priorities in order," Holmgren told the sports columnist from The Milwaukee Sentinel in his parked car at Lambeau Field while waiting for somebody to open up the place. "They are my faith, my family, and my job.

"This job isn't going to consume me. I mean, I'm going to do a good job, and I'm going to work as hard as anybody. But I'm not going to sleep at the office, and I'm not going to allow my staff to sleep there."

While the N.F.L. scientists talk about winners out-coaching losers, Holmgren would teach the game. The Packers, a team that had written the book on self-destruction, would be taught to play better.

When Lombardi took a 1-10-1 Packer team and turned it into a dynasty, the game got a message. All

Bart Starr coached the Packers for 8 seasons but only won 53 games.

coaches understand X's and O's. Some just understand them a lot better than others.

Holmgren had worked under some of the registered foxes of the game. He was an assistant at Brigham Young under LaVelle Edwards, then with San Francisco under Bill Walsh, then as offensive coordinator of the 49ers.

He would take a touch of this, a smidgen of that, spice it up with his own creativity and salt it away with plenty of sweat. The result was his own winning offense.

When he was with the 49ers, they won two Super Bowls and had two dominant players named Joe Montana and Jerry Rice. His new assignment at Green Bay was entirely different in that he took over a team best described as an emotional and physical wreck.

"My main thing is setting a standard," Holmgren said. "We'll play to a certain standard, regardless of the opponent, the site, the weather. If our players play to that standard, and the other team is better, they are better.

"Eventually, because of the draft and the resources they've got here, we should be more than competitive. I know the situation here is a good one."

So, here came Mike Holmgren. Could he do it? Was this the coach who finally could put it all together? Was he a savior?

At first glance, Holmgren looked good. He came from a winning organization. He had paid his dues.

But how did you really know what to do? After the shine wore off, would Holmgren have the fire and know-how to rebuild a team that had grown stagnant and incompetent? Could he pump life into a cadaver at Lambeau Field?

As a sportswriter assigned to cover the Packers, I had been watching this organization try to find the right man for the job since Lombardi stepped down as head coach following the 1967 season. I always had this uneasy feeling as each coach arrived and left. They all seemed like the same guy.

Look at them. They were all mediocre coaches. They all were interchangeable. They all resigned and/or were fired and moved on.

But, at the time they were appointed as the new head coach of the Packers, they surely said the right things. Promises. Always promises.

It started with Phil Bengtson. He had coached the Packer defense nine years under Lombardi. At age 54, Bengtson was hand-picked by His Highness to succeed him as head coach. He had no chance to win.

"The best I can do is stay even," Bengtson said about the impossible task of following Lombardi. Three years later, after the Packers slipped to a last-place tie with the Chicago Bears, Bengtson resigned.

Dan Devine, 46, came from the University of Missouri to succeed Bengtson at Green Bay in 1971. Although he was a very successful college coach, he was not cut out to be head coach and general manager of an N.F.L. team.

"I'm not naive enough to say we're going to burn up the league," Devine said after signing a five-year contract to coach the Packers. "But we're going to think we can whether we can or not. If a few players need convincing, we'll convince them. I didn't come here to lay an egg."

Devine's first team in Green Bay in 1971 was a 4-8-2 rotten egg. The next year, the Packers won the N.F.C. Central Division with a 10-4 record but were stopped cold by the Washington Redskins, 16-3, in the first round of the playoffs. After two third-place finishes, the Packers paid off the final year (1975) of Devine's contract without knowing he had signed a contract to coach Notre Dame.

On Christmas Eve 1974, the Packers took a gamble and named Bart Starr, 40, as head coach and general manager of the team. The Packers' great quarterback had only one previous coaching job. After retiring after 16 years as a player, he agreed to serve as quarterback coach under Devine. He asked the Packers for a three-year head coaching contract, and he asked the fans for their prayers and patience.

"I'll guarantee you one thing," Starr said of his appointment. "This will be a team you can be damn proud to root for."

Proud? Starr's teams finished 4-10, 5-9, 4-10, 8-7-1, 5-11-0, 5-10-1, 8-8, 6-4-1 and 8-8. On Christmas Eve 1983, Starr no longer was the people's choice and was fired.

Forrest Gregg, 50, said he wanted to return to Green Bay and coach the Packers. So the man who had coached the Cincinnati Bengals to Super Bowl XVI, signed a five-year contract on Dec. 24, 1984, after he was quickly released from his contract by Paul Brown of the Bengals.

"I'm not a prophet, so I can't tell you what is

Forrest Gregg's record was a dismal 25-37-1.

going to happen," Gregg said. "But I can tell you that I didn't take this job to field a losing team. I took this job to field a winning team. That will happen."

Gregg could never get the Packers over the hump. His teams finished two years with the same 8-8 record. Following a 4-12 season in 1986 and a 5-9-1 campaign in 1987, Gregg abruptly quit to take a job as head coach at his alma mater, Southern Methodist.

Nineteen days later, Lindy Infante, the 47-year-old offensive coordinator with the Cleveland Browns, signed a five-year contract to coach the Packers after Michigan State coach George Perles had turned them down.

"I didn't take this job to be here two or three years and go out a loser," Infante said. His team pulled off a 10-4 record in 1989, but overall he was 24-40. The Packers fired him three days before Christmas with three years remaining on his contract.

On Jan. 11, 1992, Mike Holmgren, the 43-year-old offensive coordinator from the 49ers, signed a five-year contract to coach the Packers, attempting to succeed where five had failed trying to follow the legacy of Lombardi. He offered no predictions other than to say he would work very hard to get the team turned around and headed in the right direction.

Many observers felt Holmgren would get his comeuppance in the rough-and-tumble N.F.L. Not experienced enough to be head coach. Wasn't the last coach an offensive coordinator? Holmgren's West Coast offense would not work in the frigid climes of Wisconsin.

When Holmgren accepted the job, he annouced that he looked at himself as a teacher. A dozen years earlier he was an obscure assistant high school coach who also taught history in San Jose, Calif.

Holmgren also was a student. He studied coaches and Lombardi was the one he studied.

"Living up to Lombardi, I'm not sure anyone will

be able to do that, so it doesn't bother me so much," Holmgren said. "My main concern is getting better every week, coaching a young quarterback and fielding a consistent team."

He said he was not a yeller and a screamer on the field; but because of the way he teaches, he would get everyone's attention.

We all know what successful coaches are suppose to look and sound like. Take Vince Lombardi, the greatest professional coach of them all. Gap-toothed, bull-necked, a voice like an iron foundry, a volcanic temper, he was born to be a football coach.

Now, check out Mike Holmgren. He looks like your favorite uncle with husky jowls, soft blue eyes and a bushy mustache. He rarely cusses. He looks kind, unflappable, full of understanding. But beneath that sunny veneer is pure football coach.

The Packers' version of Coming Attractions was about to be unveiled. At the team's first mini-camp in April, Mike Holmgren was on center stage.

If he could win at Green Bay, he would be hailed as the greatest person to hit town since Lombardi. If he lost? Well, he would join the list of five others who tried their hand at this, failed, and left town in a hurry.

That's pressure. How does it feel?

Mike Holmgren smiled. "I'm ready for this," he said.

He arrived with all the intention of lighting a flame under the Packers. In Brett Favre and Reggie White, he soon found the ideal blowtorches.

All Holmgren did was to breathe sweet life into a franchise that was a little too saturated with losing. In four years he had transformed the Packers from a 4-12 status into one of the strongest contending teams in the N.F.L. He had strung together four consecutive winning seasons, three straight playoff berths, the Packers' first outright division title in 23 years and came within one game of the Super Bowl.

Vince Lombardi's 5 N.F.L. titles spoiled Packers fans.

Now every die-hard fan who swore the Packers made a mistake choosing an offensive coordinator from San Francisco as their head coach, as they did when they selected Infante from Cleveland, couldn't say enough good things about this transplanted Californian. Nor could his boss.

"I believe the relationship I have with Mike Holmgren is such that I wouldn't trade that for any coach in the N.F.L.," Wolf said. "He has taken a ragamuffin football team and made it respected throughout the league, and most importantly the division."

Holmgren says he is not a complex man but just a guy who is coaching football. He is not a control freak. But he believes in discipline, in being on time.

It's that simple.

Mike Holmgren simple? Sure, and so is his offense. Try to convince defensive coordinators around the N.F.L. on that one.

Almost every player in Green Bay during the Holmgren era knows the coach's temper and lack of patience for stupid mistakes. At 6-foot-5, his presence on the field and sideline can be overwhelming.

"He doesn't just say it," former Packer nose tackle John Jurkovich said. "You can feel it. If you drop passes or fumble or jump offside, you cannot play on this team."

In a game against the Minnesota Vikings, on Nov. 5, 1995, in the Metrodome, Favre and backup quarterback Ty Detmer both went out with injuries and in came T.J. Rubley, a third-stringer. With one minute to play and the score tied, 24-24, the Packers had the ball on the Viking 38 and all they needed from Rubley was another yard or two to set up a potential winning field goal from Chris Jacke.

Rubley made an unthinkable pass, a flip back across his body into traffic. The ball was intercepted by Vikings linebacker Jeff Brady, and Minnesota moved in for a field goal and a 27-24 victory.

"I called a quarterback sneak," Holmgren said. "He changed the play. He thought he had the choice."

Two weeks later, Rubley was released. "I don't think I ever had a coach that upset," he said.

Much like Lombardi's "Run to Daylight" system, Holmgren emphasizes a "Pass to Daylight" attack that has Favre on a record-breaking pace.

"I'm doing what I'm coached to do, and I'm doing it well," Favre said. "If I heard Mike say it once, I've heard him say it a million times: 'Let the system work for you.' If I would do that I would complete every pass."

Such confidence reveals a locker room belief in Holmgren that goes beyond X's and O's.

One of the reasons losing never stopped in Green Bay under previous regimes was because the coaches would beat the players to death in practice. Starr ran tough practices and Gregg might have conducted the toughest practices in the league.

On Friday, Gregg's teams worked on goal-line and short-yardage plays in which the tempo was expected to be crisp. Linebacker Brian Noble remembered plowing into blockers and running backs from a running start less than 48 hours before kickoff. "I dreaded Fridays," Noble said.

Holmgren's teams hit less in practice at Green Bay than any since those coached by Lombardi, who all but eliminated contact work once the season began. "I don't need to bang all the time to see how tough guys are," the coach said.

While Lombardi succeeded with an iron-fist in his day — "he treats us all alike, like dogs," Henry Jordan said — Holmgren succeeds with a softer touch. He regularly listens to a players committee. He chased tight end Keith Jackson down in Arkansas when the free agent was considering other offers. He visited Favre in Kansas during his rehabilitation from pain-killing drug dependency. He practically spoke for Favre in dealing with that matter when the quarterback returned to training camp.

"Above all, he is fair. He yells at me and Reggie and other players think, 'If he yells at Reggie, he can yell at us,' " defensive end Sean Jones said.

For 30 years, the Packers have had to live with the Ghost of Lombardi, never having made it back to the Super Bowl.

It was like a curse.

It forced five coaches to leave Green Bay. None of them could convince the N.F.L. or the Packer organization that a title contender could be built here.

This community-run operation was an antiquated enterprise. To prevent this franchise from being rudderless, the Packers have restructured their foot-

Holmgren's brilliant offense and a gutsy defense have been the keys to the Packers' turnaround.

ball operations with strong leadership with the addition of Ron Wolf and Mike Holmgren and it has finally paid off.

"We were always criticized for people we hired to run this team," Harlan said.

"They would always say, 'Why do you expect them to win in Green Bay because they have never won before?' Ron Wolf and Mike Holmgren have been to the Super Bowl with their respective teams and have won it."

The pressure of winning a championship is fueling this team. This team has its own identity, the right chemistry and attitude, and the perfect coach.

Don't think for a moment the old guard hasn't noticed. Each autumn the alumni gather for a homecoming game at Lambeau Field, and members of Green Bay's Super Bowl I and II of 1966 and '67 were honored Sept.15. They were warmly received, but the biggest cheers were directed at Holmgren's Heroes who destroyed the San Diego Chargers, 42-10.

Dave Robinson, a linebacker who played for the Packers during the Glory Years, explained. "Unlike the other coaches who have followed Lombardi,

Mike Holmgren has done a heck of a job being able to live with the Ghost of Lombardi. He doesn't try to fight it, overcome or out-do it. That feeling permeates throughout the organization. The old guys love these Packers, and the new guys embrace us. It's one team — the Green Bay Packers. Winners."

James Lofton, an All-Pro wide receiver who played under Starr and Gregg, said he didn't know if the Lombardi Mystique had anything to do with the lack of success when he was at Green Bay.

"This team really has personnel," Lofton said. "They have the league's most valuable player (Favre). They have the defense — two of the all-time sack leaders in Reggie White and Sean Jones. The secondary is playing extremely well. This is a very solid football team.

"And their ace in the hole is the fact Nike has brought Lombardi back to life. You see him on those TV commercials during every game. And Brett Favre wears Nike."

Forget Lombardi? Never. But from day one, with every game, it has become increasingly evident that Mike Holmgren has escaped the Old Man's shadow. He is a ghostbuster and coach to be reckoned with.

Ten to reme

mber

1 **PACKERS 28, LIONS 24**
JANUARY 8, 1994

2 **PACKERS 16, LIONS 12**
DECEMBER 31, 1994

3 **PACKERS 35, BEARS 28**
NOVEMBER 12, 1994

4 **PACKERS 24, STEELERS 19**
DECEMBER 24, 1995

5 **PACKERS 37, FALCONS 20**
DECEMBER 31, 1995

6 **PACKERS 27, 49ers 17**
JANUARY 6, 1996

7 **COWBOYS 38, PACKERS 27**
JANUARY 14, 1996

8 **PACKERS 39, EAGLES 13**
SEPTEMBER 9, 1996

9 **PACKERS 42, CHARGERS 10**
SEPTEMBER 15, 1996

10 **PACKERS 23, 49ers 20**
OCTOBER 14, 1996

The Packers' defense swarms to stop the Lions' Barry Sanders

Sharpe Answers 'Prayer'

Late TD Moves Pack Into 2nd Round Playoffs

By Pete Dougherty

Green Bay Press-Gazette

PONTIAC, MI — Wayne Fontes called it a heave, Mike Holmgren called it the play of the game, and most everybody called it a great throw.

| Packers | 28 |
| Lions | 24 |

With a minute five seconds to play and the Packers down a field goal, Brett Favre put his exceptionally strong throwing arm to use, throwing a bomb across his body and across the field to a wide-open Sterling Sharpe. The 40-yard touchdown pushed the Packers past the Detroit Lions, 28-24, and into the second round of the playoffs.

"That was a huge play for this organization," said Steve Mariucci, the quarterbacks coach.

The play was remarkably similar to one he had misfired to Mark Clayton just a series before.

The situation was the same — Detroit led, 24-21 — with about 7½ minutes to play. As he had much of the day, Favre scrambled, eventually breaking to his right. When Clayton slipped well behind defensive back William White, Favre fired on the run, but his long throw drifted out of bounds.

"I thought, 'There's our chance, and I blew it,' " he said.

Six minutes later, he faced a tougher throw against his body, but that might have played to his advantage. When he scrambled to his left, defensive back Kevin Scott, who was covering Sharpe along the right sideline, didn't go with the receiver toward the end zone.

Scott described the mistake as a miscommunication in the defensive backfield because of the crowd noise at the Pontiac Silverdome. But he also admitted, "He was scrambling to the other side. I wasn't even thinking of him throwing it over there."

"It was pretty far," general manager Ron Wolf said. "(Denver's John) Elway could probably do that. But I don't know how many guys could."

When the ball finally came down in Sharpe's arms in the corner of the end zone: "Time stopped for a minute," Scott said. "I was kind of in awe."

It was a huge play for Favre after he had thrown four interceptions in a 30-20 loss to the Lions just last week. He completed 15 of 26 passes for 204 yards and had moments like he has had much of the season.

In the third quarter he forced a pass to Sharpe deep in Packers territory that Melvin Jenkins intercepted and returned 15 yards for a Lions touchdown. The very next series he threw a bullet to a well-covered Sharpe for a 28-yard Packers score, and later still he threw the game-winning bomb.

"It was a come-from-behind win, a big game, a lot on the line," Mariucci said. "He had some ups and downs and played through it. I think it's one of his

Brett Favre's 40-yard TD to Sterling Sharpe gave the Packers a 28-24 win.

Detroit's Derrick Moore stumbles into the end zone for a Lions' TD.

very best games overall."

Said Lions safety Harry Colon: "I give him credit. He played awful last week and came back and played decent this week. He played good enough to win."

Jenkins' touchdown was Favre's only interception of the day and the 25th he has thrown this season.

Favre's last pass made the interception a footnote, though.

"I don't want to say a hope and a prayer, but that's really what it was," Favre said. "I knew where Sterling was going to be and he knew not to give up on me, because who knows where I'll throw it. Sometimes I never know."

Said Wolf: "I don't care if he throws 36 interceptions, I think he's the best quarterback in the Central Division, and I think that's why we're still playing."

Somehow, This Team Finds a Way to Bounce Back

By Kevin Isaacson

Green Bay Press-Gazette

They bounce back. They are not the most talented, most popular or certainly the most healthy players in the National Football League, but the Green Bay Packers must be the most resilient.

"We've bounced back a lot this season," Coach Mike Holmgren said. "I didn't know if we had any bounce left."

It has been a season of unbelievable peaks and valleys.

After a 1-3 start, three straight wins. After a turnover-laden Monday night loss at Kansas City, three more wins.

After quarterback Brett Favre's 21-point give-away at Chicago, a strong showing on a Sunday night in San Diego. After falling to 0-4 against Vikings coach Dennis Green, a playoff-clinching victory against the Raiders.

No matter how low it seemed to go, they always bounced back.

But even Holmgren started to wonder Saturday, after Favre threw his 25th interception and the Lions returned it for a touchdown and a 17-7 lead.

"I wasn't feeling real great," he said.

Running back Darrell Thompson romps through the middle of the Detroit defense.

Neither was Favre, until Lions linebacker Chris Spielman tried to make him feel worse.

Spielman, the emotional leader of the Lions defense, had ripped Favre in the Detroit media after his four interceptions in last week's 30-20 loss. This time, as Green Bay's quarterback lay face down in the end zone, he offered his comments in person.

"They were telling me, 'We're going to be on you all day,' " Favre said.

It was exactly what the ultra-competitive quarterback need to hear.

"I'm thinking to myself, Don't go over there and start signaling No. 1's to your fans just yet,' " Favre said.

Four completions later, Favre had bounced back and with him the Packers bounced back. One minute, Sterling Sharpe was celebrating his second touchdown catch, the next rookie George Teague his record 101-yard interception return.

The Lions regained the lead, breathing life back into a Silverdome crowd quelled by Teague's touchdown. But their celebration was again premature, and served only to sweeten the outcome for the Packers.

"To come in here, with this kind of adversity," general manager Ron Wolf said, "this is very, very special."

Especially so for Favre. After the interception, he completed nine of his 11 passes for 138 yards and two touchdowns.

"Everybody had wrote me off," Favre said. "But I showed them."

So did the Packers. Six days ago an underachieving 9-7 team, they're one of only eight teams remaining in the N.F.L. playoffs after this weekend's games.

Edgar Bennett looks for an opening in the Lions' defense.

Lions Weep Today

Packers' Defense Holds Sanders to Only 13 Yards

By Pete Dougherty

Green Bay Press-Gazette

GREEN BAY — This was like holding Michael Jordan scoreless in an N.B.A. game.

In the Green Bay Packers' most impressive defensive performance of the season Saturday, they did the unthinkable. They held Barry Sanders, the N.F.L.'s premier running back, to negative yardage rushing.

| Packers | 16 |
| Lions | 12 |

He had 13 carries but managed to get past the line of scrimmage on only six of them in the Packers' 16-12 win over the Lions in a wild-card playoff game at Lambeau Field.

He had minus-one yard rushing on the day, and if his three pass receptions are included, he gained three yards total on the 16 plays he got the ball. The Packers went after him without exception.

"I think I saw something I've never seen in my five of six years in the N.F.L.," Packers safety LeRoy Butler said. "I saw some good (hits) on Barry Sanders. No one ever gets good shots on him."

The Packers moved on to the second round of the playoffs by playing more like they did in the first half of the season than the scoring machine they've been in the second.

They ran an offense without injured receiver Sterling Sharpe that was on the conservative side and, importantly, committed no turnovers. And they left it to their defense to keep the score down and then make a final stand in the last two minutes to clinch the win.

It was much like several games in September and October, when their defense climbed to No. 1 in the N.F.L. rankings before struggling in November.

They had pulled out tight games against Minnesota (16-10), the Los Angeles Rams (24-17), and even more recently the game against the Lions (38-30), when they wouldn't give up the end zone on late drives that got well into their own territory.

Quarterback Brett Favre took advantage of great field position in the fourth quarter to lead a drive for a crucial 28-yard field goal by Chris Jacke. That bumped the lead from three points to six with 5½ minutes to play, and meant the Lions had to get more than a field goal to stay in the game.

Then the defense held inside its own 20, with Bryce Paup sacking Dave Krieg on third down, and the secondary pushing 6-foot-4 receiver Herman Moore to a catch just out of the end zone on fourth down.

"The offense tears the ticket when you come in, but the defense has to win games," Butler said.

The key, though, was clamping Sanders. He had been the difference the last time the teams

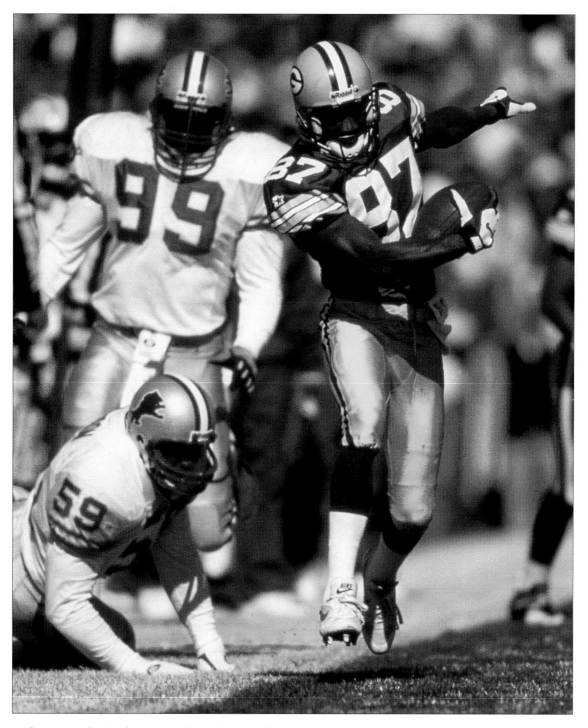

Robert Brooks (87) tiptoes the sidelines following a pass reception.

Sean Jones (96) and Don Davey (99) apply pressure to Detroit quarterback Dave Krieg.

played by gaining 188 yards in the Lions' 34-31 victory a month ago.

In that game, Reggie White played almost exclusively at defensive left end, in part because that position didn't force him to use his injured left arm as much as anywhere else along the line. But then the Lions took him out of the game by running Sanders to the Packers' right on 15 of 20 carries.

But Saturday, defensive coordinator Fritz

middle (of the field)."

With White and John Jurkovic in the middle, and Don Davey and Sean Jones at the ends, the Packers didn't give Sanders any openings all day. Sanders' longest run from scrimmage was for seven yards, and he was dropped for losses on six carries.

Not only did Sanders rush for negative yardage, but the Lions were minus-four yards for the game on the ground, which is an N.F.L. playoff record for fewest in a game.

"Since I've been here as head coach, no team has dominated us on the line of scrimmage (like today)," Detroit's Wayne Fontes said.

Sanders this year had the fourth-best season rushing in N.F.L. history (1,883 yards), though he has had difficult games. The Minnesota Vikings held him to 16 yards on 12 carries early in the season, and the Lions lost, 10-3. In fact, Detroit won only one of his six worst rushing games this year.

Like the Vikings' attacking defense in that early game, the Packers went right after Sanders.

"We said, 'When you've got your shot, take it,' " Shurmur said. "The worst thing you can do is sit there and let him juke you because he'll break your ankles."

The Packers will go to their next playoff game, either at San Francisco or Dallas with a defense that's played better lately. It has allowed an average of only 12.3 points the last four games after a November slumber in which it gave up 29 points or more three times.

"In Miami on Jan. 29 (at the Super Bowl), when they're talking about the two teams playing football, they won't be talking about the Green Bay Packers holding Barry Sanders to minus yards," Jones said. "Without being flip, until we get to the Super Bowl these things are just steps along the road."

Shurmur played White mostly in the interior of the defensive line, at either tackle position.

"It's easier to get away from (White) when he's an outside guy," Shurmur said.

"Kind of like if you want to stay away from a *cornerback* you throw away from him. But it's hard to take a safety out of the game because he's in the

Sanders Given No Room to Run

By Tony Walter

Green Bay Press-Gazette

The best running back in football went backwards Saturday afternoon.

Barry Sanders and negative rushing yardage have never been a match.

Yet, there it was, as clear as the print on the game statistics sheet.

Barry Sanders and minus-1 yard rushing.

For the first time ever, the incomparable Sanders actually subtracted from his career rushing total in the course of a complete game.

He carried the ball 13 times. On more than half of the carries, he didn't gain yardage.

He caught three passes for 4 yards.

Coach Wayne Fontes, without an explanation for the Lions' failure to spring Sanders, knew the impact of the surprising statistic.

"We're learning little by little that when Barry Sanders isn't having the kind of game we expect him to have, it's hard for this team to win," said Fontes.

Sanders wasn't aware of his rushing total as he prepared to climb on the team bus after the game.

But he knew the Packers defense, which he had chewed up just four weeks ago, mastered him.

"They just did a good job of pursuing," said the soft-spoken Sanders. "When we tried to get outside, they were always there and did a good job of fighting off the blocks and closing up all the gaps in the defense."

Sanders, who rushed for 1,883 yards in the regular season, said the field wasn't his excuse either.

"It wasn't ideal, but I think more than anything was the fact that they played real good. That's the best they've played (against the Lions) this year," he said.

Reggie White gave Packers fans a #1 salute before the game.

Sanders carried the ball three times in the Lions' first offensive series. He was tackled for a 2-yard loss by Doug Evans and George Koonce, then gained 7-yards off left end.

But on third down, Don Davey broke through to throw Sanders for a 6-yard loss, and the trend was begun.

Sanders didn't meet with reporters following the game. He dressed in a side room, did a national television interview, then headed for the team bus.

Ice Bowl Now Just a Memory

By Chris Havel

Green Bay Press Gazette

No. It wasn't the Ice Bowl. Nothing could be. Yet in several ways, the Green Bay Packers' 16-12 victory over Detroit in Saturday's N.F.C. wild-card playoff game was better.

Better because it represents the next logical step for a franchise on the rise, not the crowning achievement in a decade of superiority.

Better because it allows a city and its fans to cherish the past without being forced to live in it by a perennial laughingstock.

Better because it is here and now, not way-back-when.

Better for many reasons, the most important being this: The Packers are no longer some fly-by-night, butt-of-everyone's-jokes-outfit. Those days, like the Ice Bowl, are in the past.

This is a living, breathing, bona fide team to be reckoned with.

The N.F.L.'s so-called experts might sneer at the suggestion. Fine. They'll be the same folks begging for a press box seat at Lambeau Field when the Packers host an N.F.C. divisional playoff game next year.

This isn't the over-reaction of some wide-eyed diehard who's gotten carried away after too much New Year's Eve merriment.

It's reality.

For a second straight season, the Packers are among the N.F.L.'s Elite Eight. They're still playing while 20 other teams are forced to watch and wonder. Think it's easy? Think again.

Only two others — Dallas and San Francisco — have returned from last year.

Buffalo, Kansas City, Houston, the Raiders and Giants fell by the wayside. OK. In the Oilers' case, fell off the planet.

Ask yourself which roster would you trade the Packers for in the entire league. The 49ers? Sure. The Cowboys? OK, but only if Barry Switzer and Jerry Jones aren't part of the bargain.

That's it.

Now ask yourself which quarterback you'd rather have than Brett Favre: Steve Young? Troy Aikman? Drew Bledsoe?

Maybe. Maybe not. The debate might be long, but the list is short.

Favre was born to play here. He's a blue collar, shot-and-a-beer QB. OK. Maybe a multiple shot-and-beer QB. Any way you pour it, the guy's a big-time quarterback minus the big-time attitude.

Reggie White believes.

Asked if this team gives him the best chance of any he's been on to reach the Super Bowl, he said yes.

The reason: "Brett Favre."

"I think we've got a quarterback who can take us there," said White.

Favre completed 23 of 28 passes for 262 yards and no interceptions. The numbers would've been better if not for three drops by Anthony Morgan. Impressive, considering Sterling Sharpe didn't play.

Even more impressive considering Favre was sick for two days this week with a stomach ailment.

"With the car wreck I had (in college) and the intestine I had taken out, occasionally I'll have some blockage up there. There's no cure. No medication to take. Just tough it out. Just let it pass."

Two gutty performances in one week. Now that's impressive.

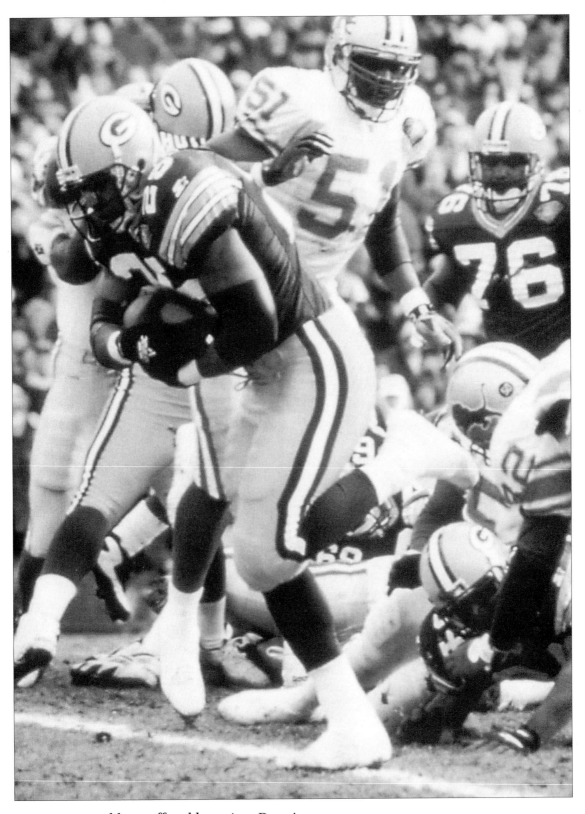

Dorsey Levens blasts off tackle against Detroit.

Win Ensures Tie for No. 1

Favre's 3 TD's Lead Pack Over Bears

By Pete Dougherty

Green Bay Press-Gazette

GREEN BAY — As Brett Favre stood beneath the stands waiting to be introduced to the Lambeau Field crowd Sunday, he told a teammate, "I haven't had butterflies like this in my stomach for a long time."

Packers	35
Bears	28

Those butterflies indicated how compelled Favre was to play quarterback for the Packers against Chicago on Sunday despite the badly sprained ankle that kept his status uncertain all week.

The Packers, losers of their previous two games, were either going to regain a share of the N.F.C. Central Division lead or drop all the way back to .500 after a promising 5-2 start. Favre's butterflies also indicated he was ready to play, because he responded with one of the best games of his professional career in the Packers' 35-28 win at Lambeau Field.

"He hadn't had two of the best games in the world in the last couple weeks," receiver Mark Ingram said.

"He's just a competitor and he wanted to come in and have a good game. That's what champions are made of."

The win tied the Packers with the Bears for first place in the division at 6-4, and gave the Packers a huge edge over Chicago.

The season sweep means they will win any head-to-head tiebreaker with the Bears.

Plus, even after losing the previous two weeks, the Packers are tied with five other teams for the second-best record in the N.F.C. behind 8-2 Dallas.

"We're in the driver's seat in the division," linebacker George Koonce said. "If we keep winning, if we win our next two division games, we're division champs."

How good was Favre on Sunday? He threw for a season-best in yards (336) and completion percentage (25-for-33, 75.8 percent), and his five touchdown passes tied the Packers' record set by Cecil Isbell in 1942 and tied by Lynn Dickey twice ('81, '83) and Don Horn once ('69).

Those totals, combined with no interceptions, gave him a 147.2 passer rating for the day out of a maximum 158.3 points. That's a remarkable 6.8 point jump for his season rating from 83.0 to 89.8.

Because of his severely sprained ankle, Favre had been unable to practice all week except for Friday, when he did some one-on-one fundamentals work with Coach Mike Holmgren, and Saturday, when he took a few snaps during half-speed passing drills.

Several of Favre's teammates said that by midweek they thought he would play. Favre, though, said he didn't know for sure until Saturday night.

On Sunday, he had the ankle heavily taped, "like a cast," he said. His mobility was limited but he still managed to have one of his best games ever.

Robert Brooks had a career day against Chicago: 6 passes for 138 yards and 2 TD's.

There actually were indications he might be especially sharp this week. Steve Mariucci, the Packers' quarterbacks coach, gives the quarterbacks rapid-fire quizzes on Saturdays. He said Favre's answers were "bang, bang, bang. I was trying to get him to say something wrong, and he was sharp as a tack. He probably studied more this week than usual because he couldn't do the physical stuff."

Favre helped give the Packers a big boost by matching Chicago quarterback Erik Kramer pass for pass at the start of the game. Both went 5-for-5 in taking their team to a touchdown on their first possession, but the Packers got the bigger lift, because "Brett was back," fullback Dorsey Levens said.

Favre won the shootout, though Kramer also had

a good day: 23-for-38 passing for 318 yards, two touchdowns and one interception.

The field, slippery from recent snow and cold weather, appeared to help the offenses, as defensive backs from both teams slipped several times. That helped make it a day of big plays, with each team completing five passes for 21 yards or more.

Packers receiver Robert Brooks had the most productive game of his career, catching six passes for a career-best 138 yards and two touchdowns. His second touchdown was especially big because it answered a Bears' score that had given them a 28-21 lead late in the third quarter.

The Bears, who blitzed more as the game wore on, blitzed on the first play after that go-ahead touchdown. But fullback Dorsey Levens picked off linebacker Vinson Smith in front of Favre — in the first half Smith snuffed a Packers' drive when he slipped past Levens for a sack — and Favre lofted a deep pass for Brooks for a 44-yard score.

"I was looking for it the second time around," Levens said of the blitz.

Said Brooks: "We felt we had to score quickly to get the momentum back. Once we did, the crowd got into it, and our defense stepped it up."

Though the offenses dominated this day — the teams combined for 800 total yards — the Packers' defense held the lead in the final minutes. After Edgar Bennett's 16-yard touchdown on a screen pass with 9:17 to play, Chicago got the ball twice trailing, 35-28.

Safety LeRoy Butler ended the first drive by intercepting Kramer in the end zone on fourth-and-two with just under two minutes to play.

The second ended when the Packers forced three incompletions in the end zone in the final 11 seconds with Chicago at the Packers' 14.

"We're back," Butler said. "We've licked our wounds and they've healed."

Playing with a bad ankle, Brett Favre threw for 5 TD's to lead the Packers to a 35-28 win.

Late Stands Bail Out Defense

By Pete Dougherty

Green Bay Press-Gazette

The Packers struggled much of Sunday trying to slow down one of the N.F.L.'s most productive offenses. But they did make the defensive stops when the game was on the line.

In a 35-28 win over Chicago at Lambeau Field, the Packers' problems stopping the run continued, as they gave up 140 yards on 33 carries.

The Bears came into the game with the No. 2 offense in the N.F.L. in points scored and No. 6 in total yards, and they showed why. Their 28 points and 444 yards were the second-most the Packers have given up this year behind the 34 points and 448 yards Dallas had on Oct. 8.

The Packers' defense, though, made the seven-point lead stand up by stopping Chicago on its final two drives inside the Packers' 25.

"We shouldn't be asking our offense to score 35 points for us every week to win," linebacker George Koonce said. "We need to tighten up a little bit, especially on the run."

In the last six games, the Packers have given up an average of 127 yards rushing a game. In the previous four, they had given up an average of 84.5 yards.

Chicago's Robert Green and Rashaan Salaam combined for 122 yards rushing. Green had 68 yards on 16 carries (4.3 yard average), and Salaam 54 yards on 13 carries (4.2 yard average).

"We just can't figure out what the problem is right now," said defensive end Reggie White, who played most of the game despite having a strained ligament in his knee. "We've got to find out what the problem is because this is the most important stretch right here."

The Bears proved their high offensive rankings are not a fluke with an impressive passing game featuring quarterback Erik Kramer and receivers Curtis Conway and Jeff Graham.

Kramer, who is having an excellent season, completed 23 of 38 passes for 318 yards. His two touchdown passes gave him 23 for the season, which is one more than the Packers' Brett Favre.

Conway and Graham each went over the 100-yard mark receiving — Conway with six receptions for 126 yards and Graham with seven for 108.

Conway had three receptions of 21 yards or more, including a 46-yarder for a touchdown that tied the game at 21 with seven seconds left in the first half. Conway beat rookie Craig Newsome and safety LeRoy Butler on the play and got a perfectly placed pass from Kramer, who has the reputation for being one of the N.F.L.'s most accurate passers on long throws.

"That was inexcusable to me," Packers coach Mike Holmgren said. "There wasn't much time left, we were in man coverage and there was a safety in the hole. We just didn't take real good angles on it. How many choices do you have with 11 seconds left?"

The Packers, though, did sack Kramer twice, which is unusual. He has been the most difficult quarterback in the league to sack

Edgar Bennett stretches out to cross the goal line for a TD against the Bears.

while operating in an offense where he throws quickly off short dropbacks. Combined with their two sacks of him when the teams met in the second week of the season, the Packers have four of the seven sacks the Bears have yielded this year.

Defensive end Sean Jones and White shared the first sack, and Butler had the second for an 11-yard loss on a safety blitz in the second quarter.

Butler also intercepted Kramer in the end zone late in the fourth quarter with the Packers leading, 35-28. On fourth-and-two from the Packers' 22, Kramer overthrew well-covered tight end Ryan Wetnight and Butler made the diving interception with 1:53 to play.

Later, the Bears drove to the Packers' 14 with 11 seconds to play. Kramer threw three passes into the end zone, but none came close to connecting, with Evans covering Graham on one play; Lenny McGill and George Teague covering Michael Timpson on the second; and Butler covering Timpson on the third.

"The game's on the line right there, that's why it's fun, in a way — as long as you win," Teague said. "But you really don't want it to come down to that."

Favre Leads, Packers Follow

By Chris Havel

Green Bay Press-Gazette

First, Brett Favre walked. Then, he walked on water.

The Green Bay Packers' quarterback was Moses with a limp, relying on a pass after pass Sunday to part the Bears' secondary as if it were the Red Sea.

By the time he stepped onto his sore left ankle and into his fifth touchdown pass of the Packers' 35-28 victory, the Bears had to wonder if Favre's miracles — and the Lambeau Field humiliation — will never cease.

"Favre did a heckuva job under the circumstances," sighed Dave Wannstedt, whose postgame mood matched Favre's ankle. Both were sore and blue.

The Bears' head coach has now lost five of six games to the Packers. Over the past three years, he's known even less success in Green Bay than he did in 1974, when an injury kept him from making the team as a late draft pick.

Green Bay just isn't Wannstedt's kind of town. It belongs to Favre, whose performances helped the Packers re-open a world of possibilities.

In one day, they went from longshot to favorite in a muddled N.F.C. Central race. They went from wild-card hopeful to nipping at the Cowboys' spurs.

Technically, the Packers and Bears, at 6-4, move into a first-place tie in the N.F.C. Central. Realistically, Green Bay holds a one-game lead because a sweep of the season series guarantees the nod in any tiebreaker.

Favre will reap much of the credit.

He completed 25 passes to nine different players for 336 yards. He hooked up with every eligible receiver that stepped into Green Bay's huddle.

Bears cornerback James Burton, subbing for the injured Donnell Woolford, said it well: "He was just Favre."

Just as Burton was, well, Burton.

Twice, Robert Brooks made the nondescript cornerback look like Deputy Dawg, leaving him scratching his head and asking, "Which way did he go?"

For that matter, the Bears' entire defensive secondary looked befuddled. Their 26th ranking among N.F.L. pass defenses seems well-deserved.

After the game, Irvin Favre stood in the Packers' locker room, beaming like a proud papa. His pride wasn't rooted in his son's play, although he modestly described it as "pretty damn good."

What pleased him most was the way the players rallied around his son.

"The line really blocked for him," Irvin Favre said. "The receivers did some amazing things, too. That's a sign that they respect him as the leader. Brett can't do it alone."

He didn't have to Sunday.

There was Anthony Morgan, whose fully extended 21-yard catch set up the Packers' third touchdown.

"You're going to perform for your leader," Morgan said. "And he performed for us."

There was the offensive line, which gave Favre enough time and combined with Edgar Bennett to execute two screens to perfection.

Packers guard Aaron Taylor (73) attempts to keep Bears rusher Chris Zorich, a former Notre Dame teammate, out of the Packers' backfield.

There was Mark Ingram, whose three catches were overshadowed by his superior judgment on an option pass. Quarterbacks with a decade of N.F.L. experience might've tried to force a throw. Ingram took the 4-yard loss.

There was Keith Jackson, who caught three passes, including two that converted third downs. For a change, he was more help than hindrance.

There was Antonio Freeman, whose returns twice set up Packers scores.

Yes, there was the Packers' defense. It didn't manage many big plays, which magnified the few big ones it did have.

There was Wayne Simmons' drivehalting hit on Robert Green and LeRoy Butler's end zone interception.

Said Butler: "I told myself. 'If this guy catches a TD, I'll be the goat.' "

Butler made the play. No goat horns in the Packers' locker room. Just a gutty QB and a bunch of teammates who were glad to lend a helping hand.

Afterward, Simmons said what a lot of people were thinking: "I sat back and I said to myself, ' No. 4. You gotta love him.' "

Lady Luck Picks Pack

Steelers Botch Last-Minute Scoring Chance

By Pete Dougherty

Green Bay Press-Gazette

GREEN BAY — Good luck, fate, whatever the name, the Packers had it Sunday with the N.F.C. Central Division title on the line.

It came in the person of Pittsburgh receiver Yancy Thigpen, who on the Steelers' very last play broke wide open in the corner of the end zone only to drop the game-winning pass.

| Packers | 24 |
| Steelers | 19 |

That left the Packers and a record Lambeau Field crowd of 60,649 spectators delirious with a 24-19 win that gave Green Bay its first outright division title since 1972.

Sixty minutes of football, and it came down to the Steelers' leading receiver dropping a routine short pass on fourth down.

"Luck goes both ways," said Sean Jones, a Packers defensive end. "Luck was the thing that gave them a good spot (on fourth down eight plays earlier). Let's start there. Sometimes your luck runs out."

The Packers' 11-5 record (.688) is their best season-ending winning percentage since 1967 (9-4-1, .692) and their most wins since 1966 (12-2). But what made this win especially important was it landed the Packers a first-round playoff game at home.

That was important enough to compel quarterback Brett Favre to add to his growing reputation as a genuine tough guy by playing most of the second half with a bruised chest suffered on a hard hit by defensive end Ray Seals. Favre, who missed only two plays, had another Pro Bowl performance, completing 23 of 32 passes for 301 yards and two more touchdowns.

"He's a warrior," running back Edgar Bennett said. "A true warrior, and an m.v.p."

Still, for the Packers to win this division title, they had to endure a tense final two minutes.

Pittsburgh trailed only 24-19 with 5½ minutes to play and 80 yards from the end zone. By the two-minute warning, the Steelers were inside the Packers' 25.

But Green Bay nearly made the game-saving play right there when defensive tackles Gilbert Brown and John Jurkovic stuffed Neil O'Donnell on a quarterback sneak on fourth-and-less-than-a-yard. The Packers celebrated immediately, thinking they had stopped him for a slight loss.

"He didn't get it, I'm telling you," Jones said. "But there was such a pile-up that the (official) on the far side of the field marked it — I don't know who has the final say, the linesman or the umpire or who, but one had it back and one had it up. They split the difference, it looked like."

That was only the start of an unusually dramatic

Mike Holmgren and Steelers coach Bill Cowher chat briefly prior to kickoff.

first-down measurement. When the officials brought out the chains, they still couldn't tell whether it was a first down. They needed several seconds to get the ball and the marker exactly in line and several more to see whether they were touching. "I still didn't think they got it," defensive end Matt LaBounty said. "You literally needed a piece of paper in there to see if it was skewed."

The Steelers eventually got to the Packers 5, where O'Donnell spiked the ball to stop the clock.

Pittsburgh, which has the second-best record in the A.F.C. at 11-5, had three downs, 29 seconds and one timeout to get the game-winning touchdown:

■ On second down, O'Donnell threw the ball away, well over Thigpen's head on a slant pattern in the end zone with cornerback Lenny McGill close behind. That play actually set up the Steelers' fourth-down call.

■ On third down, they moved Kordell Stewart from receiver to quarterback, and he tried a draw. Jones

Edgar Bennett attempts to flee the grasp of a Steelers defender.

and safety LeRoy Butler stuffed it for a one-yard loss. ∎ Then on fourth down, they again had Thigpen and McGill lined up alone on the left side.

"You just play aggressive," McGill said. "Fourth-and-six, you don't want to give up any easy quick-outs or slants. The main thing is to play aggressive and be in his face."

Thigpen started to run another slant, but then broke outside. McGill, after initially jamming him, slipped, and Thigpen was wide open. But he juggled the ball and kneed it out of his own reach.

"I beat him," Thigpen said. "I beat him so bad. I just knew it was six. It just slipped out. It just slipped through me. It hit my knee, and when it hit my knee that's when I really lost control."

Said cornerback Doug Evans: "They knew we were going to bite on anything quick. The man upstairs — we'll take it any way we can."

That ended the day for the Packers' defense against a team that had been averaging 30.1 points over its last eight games behind its solid veteran quarterback, O'Donnell, and probably the most versatile offensive player in the N.F.L., Stewart.

The Steelers were short-handed, playing without running backs Erric Pegram, Bam Morris and John L. Williams. But they did have Stewart, who besides being their third string quarterback, played mostly at receiver, catching six passes for 42 yards.

But he didn't burn the Packers on either of the two plays he lined up at quarterback, running for a total of three yards. That included a fourth-and-one option play in the first quarter that LaBounty read, forcing a quick pitch to running back Fred McAfee. Linebacker George Koonce pounced on him for no gain, ending the drive at the Packers' 37.

O'Donnell moved the Steelers effectively, operating with a lineup that usually had three receivers and regularly had four or five. He threw for 318 yards, making him only the third quarterback to top the 300-yard mark against the Packers this year.

But once in each half the Packers held the Steelers to only a field goal after they had moved inside the Green Bay 20, and the Steelers' 19 points were the fewest they've scored since a 27-9 loss to Cincinnati on Oct. 19.

"They're a good football team with a good quarterback, and they play extremely well," said Fritz Shurmur, the Packers' defensive coordinator. "(Luck) is huge. It comes down to one play. But we made a lot of plays in that (scoring) zone."

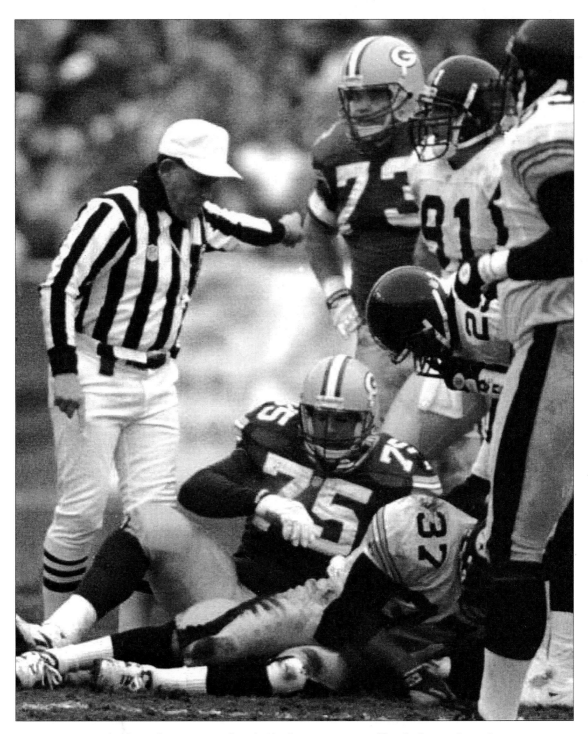

Ken Ruettgers (75) and Aaron Taylor (73) observe as an official clears the pile.

With LeRoy Butler hanging on, Pittsburgh's Kordell Stewart lunges for extra yardage.

Favre's Effort One of Blood and Guts

By Jim Hayes

Green Bay Press-Gazette

Brett Favre resembled a battered and bruised boxer who made two serious trips to the canvas Sunday.

But Favre pulled himself up off the mat before the bell rang on both occasions, and again was Green Bay's key performer as the Packers beat the Pittsburgh Steelers, 24-19, at Lambeau Field to clinch their first N.F.C. Central championship since 1972.

"I think he's a helluva quarterback," said Myron Bell, the Steelers' strong safety. "He has everything. He can scramble, he can throw the deep ball. Anything you can ask, I believe he can do."

And Favre can play with pain.

Favre, who left the game with torn ankle ligaments in a 27-24 loss to Minnesota on Nov. 5 but has started every game since, suffered a bruised chest Sunday when he was hit by Bell at the end of an eight-yard scramble to the Steelers' 1 in the third quarter.

Favre also was dazed and had to be replaced by Jim McMahon for two plays after being hit in the head by linebacker Kevin Greene on the first play of the fourth quarter.

After being hit by Bell, Favre walked to the sideline and was spiting up blood. However, he threw a touchdown pass to Mark Chmura on the following play to give the Packers a 21-10 lead while McMahon was warming up on the sideline.

Favre's two touchdown passes gave him 38 for the season, which is second to Dan Marino, who threw 48 touchdown passes in 1984 and 44 in 1986.

Drop Proves Win, Title Were Meant to Be

By Chris Havel

Green Bay Press-Gazette

This couldn't be a prelude to Super Bowl XXX. Seldom are Super Bowls so dramatic.

One moment, the Pittsburgh Steelers have victory in the bag.

The next moment — whoops! — the football inexplicably pops out of Yancey Thigpen's hands and the Green Bay Packers hold on for a 24-19 victory that secures their first N.F.C. Central Division title in 23 years.

Scarcely had Thigpen's dropped-pass tragedy turned to comedy when the comparisons began: Ah huh! So Santa Claus wears No. 82 and plays for the Steelers.

Let's hope not.

For Santa to top this boner, he'd have to wrap Rudolph and the gang around a telephone pole, or go belly up halfway down a chimney.

No. Thigpen isn't Santa. He is human.

So on behalf of the 60,649 at Lambeau Field and Packers fans throughout Green Bay and Wisconsin, "Merry Christmas, Yancey," and thank you for heeding the "Do Not Open Before Christmas" tag on that tube of stick-em.

The drop triggered an emotional scene.

There was Sean Jones, hopping on top of the Packers' bench and bringing his 6-foot-7 frame to bear on the crowd. Then with great dignity and the flair of a Shakespearean actor, he slowly bowed to the fans, a tear in his eye.

There was Reggie White, sore knee and all, trotting around Lambeau Field. It conjured up an image of Hank Aaron — White's childhood hero — circling the bases after his 715th home run. It was as if White wanted to touch 'em all.

The fans, that is.

Asked how far Green Bay will go in the playoffs, safety LeRoy Butler said, "Probably as far as Brett will take us and I think that will be real far."

Added Butler: "You see Robert (Brooks) playing with a separated shoulder. You see Brett throwing up blood on the sideline. You see the offensive lineman playing with all kinds of broken stuff. This is the toughest team I've ever played on."

"This team is special for a number of reasons," said Packers coach Mike Holmgren, the meaning of that statement transcending the words. "It was almost like, 'It should've ended that way. The way it ended.'"

Afterward, a banner was hung over Reggie White's locker with great care.

It read: *Nobody Beats Christ. Thank God 4 Reggie White. #92.*

Who knows? Maybe the Packers truly are blessed.

Doug Evans and Pittsburgh receiver Yancey Thigpen (88) chase after Thigpen's fumble.

Packers Ground Falcons

Favre's 3 TD's Set Match Against 49ers

By Pete Dougherty

Green Bay Press-Gazette

GREEN BAY — Down by a touchdown with less than three minutes into the game Sunday, the Packers still looked like a team that felt destined to beat the Atlanta Falcons in their wild card playoff matchup.

| Packers | 37 |
| Falcons | 20 |

Undaunted by Eric Metcalf's 65-yard touchdown reception just before the the 12-minute mark in the first quarter, the Packers defense kept the Falcons' dangerous run-and-shoot offense under control most of the day.

Coupled with another outstanding performance by quarterback Brett Favre that by this point in the season has become routine, the Packers soundly defeated Atlanta, 37-20, in front of a festive New Year's Eve crowd of 60, 453 spectators at Lambeau Field.

The win sets up a showdown in the second round of playoffs Saturday against the San Francisco 49ers.

"In terms of winning this game, so what?" defensive end Sean Jones said. "This is a game we expected to win. Let's go to San Francisco and see what they try to do to us."

To get to the 49ers though, the Packers had to contend with the Falcons' scary run-and-shoot led by quarterback Jeff George. The Falcons generated plenty of offense and outgained the Packers, 360 total yards to 307.

But what had set them apart this year was the play of running back Craig Heyward, their remarkably nimble 260-pound, 1,000-yard rusher. The Packers virtually took him out of the game and thus turned Atlanta into a one-dimensional attack.

Heyward, who had gained 1,083 yards and averaged a hefty 4.6 yards a carry this season, gained only 21 yards on nine carries Sunday.

That left the weight of the offense on George, who had a big day statistically without lighting up the scoreboard. He completed 30 of 54 passes for 366 yards, yet the Falcons got past the Packers' 45 on only four of their 12 possessions.

"I'm tremendously pleased with these guys," defensive coordinator Fritz Shurmur said. "Everybody's been chastising them because they haven't gotten turnovers, the statistical thing. I guess (finishing) fourth in points (allowed in the N.F.L.) isn't good enough."

Shurmur broke out a defensive package this week that he hadn't used since last year against Atlanta, an alignment of three defensive linemen and three linebackers. He used it regularly, almost always blitzing Fred Strickland from an outside lane and usually also sending Wayne Simmons or George Koonce — sometimes both — as an extra rusher.

On a sloppy surface, the Packers executed flawlessly to defeat Atlanta, 37-20.

The scheme kept the Falcons from knowing which linebackers would be rushing and also kept Strickland on the field in a game in which he otherwise wouldn't have played much. As their middle linebacker, Strickland leaves the field on passing downs, and because the run-and-shoot uses four wide receivers, the Packers were in passing-down defenses most of the day.

"We're a little short of speed rushers with Reggie (White) out," Shurmur said. "And it kind of disrupted their rhythm a little bit."

The Packers had their best day rushing the passer since White first was slowed by a sprained knee on Nov. 5. They sacked George three times, and though he occasionally had time in the pocket, he usually was under at least some duress.

"I think it worked," Koonce said. "They brought in a tight end for five snaps in the second quarter to help (with the pass protection). Then they went with the shotgun in the third quarter to keep the pressure off. I think it made him throw the ball when he didn't want to throw it."

George actually did his greatest damage on a couple plays when he was chased out of the pocket in the first half. One was the 65-yarder to Metcalf, when he scrambled right and Metcalf took off behind rookie Craig Newsome down the right sideline. Late in the first quarter saw almost a carbon copy of that play when George hit Terance Mathis on a 55-yard gain that set up a field goal.

"They were broken plays," Shurmur said. "They took three shots (deep) after that and our guys played them well."

Jones and Matt LaBounty combined for a strong day at both defensive ends. Jones had two sacks and drew a holding penalty on tackle Bob Whitfield that nullified a third-down conversion early in the second quarter.

LaBounty, starting in place of White, had four tackles, including a sack.

Favre, meanwhile, threw for only 199 yards, but was nearly flawless in completing 24 of 35 passes. He threw three touchdowns and no interceptions, which makes the Packers 20-4 in games he has started and not been intercepted.

Running back Edgar Bennett, though, might have been the key to the Packers' offense on this day. Proving again that he is outstanding in sloppy field conditions, he gained 108 yards on 24 carries, a Packers playoff record for rushing yards.

He accounted for 32 yards rushing and receiving in a fourth-quarter touchdown drive that answered a Falcons touchdown and put the Packers safely ahead at 34-17 with 7:45 to play.

"That's Mr. Shortsteps," fullback William Henderson said. "He loves it. He's got great footing. He stays on his feet in bad conditions."

Edgar Bennett — Mr. Shortsteps — rushed for a record 108 yards against Atlanta.

Mission: Next Step Is The Big One

By Chris Havel

Green Bay Press-Gazette

One week it's a Christmas present. The next week it's a New Year's Eve party. Now, it's on to San Francisco.

The Green Bay Packers once again have outlasted the holidays. If only they can find a way to last beyond the second round of the N.F.C. playoffs.

Green Bay's convincing 37-20 victory over Atlanta in Sunday's N.F.C. wildcard game means it is one of only three teams to advance to the divisional playoffs in every postseason since 1992.

That the other teams (surprise, surprise) are San Francisco and Dallas means the Packers' next step for all their steady progress under G.M. Ron Wolf and Coach Mike Holmgren, still remains their biggest step.

A victory in San Francisco on Saturday, as halfback Edgar Bennett plainly stated, "Puts us in the elite."

A lopsided loss to the 49ers — after second-round losses at Dallas in 1993 and 1994 — puts the Packers at risk of becoming a poor man's Buffalo. Going through life as someone else's stepping stone gets old fast. Just ask Jerry Quarry or any of the human punching bags who helped make Ali famous.

It is why the mere fact that there is a next week for the Packers doesn't cut it anymore. Routing the Falcons was necessary, if not necessarily difficult, but it isn't enough.

Dorsey Levens snags a TD pass.

Maybe this sounds like the tired old refrain "What have you done for me lately?" So be it. When it comes to the Packers and playoffs, what they have done lately is fall in the second round.

"Last year it was fair to say, 'Can we do it?' Until you've done it, the question still remains," Sean Jones explained.

Clearly, Jones has accumulated wisdom as well as sacks in his 12 seasons. It is why his followup to the above statement carries some weight.

"Do we have the ability to advance?" he said. "Of course we do ... This year more than last year."

Why? "We're a better team," he said. "When you execute better, you have more confidence."

Jones says that and you believe him. In the past, the Packers going to the N.F.C. Championship was more wishful thinking than honest appeal.

That is no longer the case.

Not so much because of what the Packers did to the Falcons, which was whatever they wanted to do to the Falcons, but because of what they've done all season.

There is reason to believe.

The Packers won four road games.

The closest they came to being blown out of the water was a 10-point loss at Dallas. The 49ers likely will be favored by at least that much.

"People expect San Francisco to go to the Super Bowl," LeRoy Butler said. "They don't expect us to win. We'll just play loose. We'll be willing to take more chances. That's going to be key."

Indeed, the Packers have the weapons.

"This team reminds me of the Raiders in '77," said Ken Ruettgers. "They had Kenny Stabler, a great star, like we have Brett (Favre). They had a couple defensive stars like we have. Everyone else is real solid."

Added Harry Sydney. "I think we're a more complete team right now. Last year, we tried to get a running game, but we didn't. Now we have one."

Bennett rushed for 108 yards in 24 carries for a season-best 4.5 average. He also scored a touchdown.

"He's not a mudder," said Sydney. "He's a 4-by-4. Rain. Hell. Sleet. Or snow. You know the mailman. He always gets there. Edgar has the moves."

And the Packers have the quarterback.

Asked to give three reasons why the Packers can beat the 49ers, Butler smiled and said, "Brett. Brett. Brett."

Bennett took it a step further, saying, "Offense. Defense. Special teams."

Keith Jackson believes.

"The 49ers can strike up the band and put points on the board," he said. "But we can't be in awe of what they've done. They're more vulnerable than they've been in the past."

Jackson paused and added. "Our quarterback is outstanding: our play calling has been excellent. If that keeps up, we'll be hard to beat."

Steady progress, it is said, leads to a breakthrough. If that is true, then the Packers' time should be at hand.

See you on the other side.

The Packers defense held Craig Heyward to only 21 yards on nine carries.

Defense Stars as Packers Dethrone Champs

Earns Berth in N.F.C. Title Game, First Since 1972

By Pete Dougherty

Green Bay Press-Gazette

SAN FRANCISCO — With Fritz Shurmur, Mike Holmgren and Sherman Lewis all on board, there probably never has been a team in recent years

| Packers | 27 |
| 49ers | 17 |

better prepared to play the San Francisco 49ers.

And with a defense that executed its plan superbly, along with a nearly flawless performance by m.v.p. quarterback Brett Favre, the Packers manhandled the reigning Super Bowl champions in their second round playoff game at 3Com Park on Saturday, 27-17.

The win, which is the Packers' biggest since they won the Super Bowl after the 1967 season, put them in the N.F.C. Championship game next week against the winner of the Dallas-Philadelphia game.

"(Holmgren and Lewis) have a great understanding of that offense, and you have a feel for what your guys can do," Shurmur said. "I felt reasonably good we were on track, but the guys have to still go out and do it. I thought our guys did a great job, especially our young cornerbacks."

The Packers' task was immense: Go into the home of the defending Super Bowl champs and try

to control an offense that featured two of the best players in the N.F.L., quarterback Steve Young and receiver Jerry Rice. The 49ers led the league in scoring this season and were No. 2 in total yards. And to boot they also had the league's top-ranked defense in total yards allowed and were No. 2 in points allowed.

Yet, not only did the Packers come out with a win that in and of itself is likely to open eyes around the league, they also did so in dominating fashion. They forced San Francisco into a near-desperation mentality by late in the first half, when they twice went for fourth downs. The 49ers also were in such a deep hole that they attempted a playoff-record 65 passes.

The Packers also moved the ball with startling consistency, amassing 368 total yards, the most the 49ers have given up all season, and they got at least one first down every time they touched the ball until their last possession, when the game's outcome no longer was in doubt.

"We didn't win by the skin of our teeth," linebacker George Koonce said. "Not to be bragging, but I think we won kind of convincingly."

Said general manager Ron Wolf: "People weren't willing to accept how good we are. We're pretty good."

San Francisco quarterback Steve Young was battered by the Packers' defense all afternoon.

Perhaps the key to the game was that the Packers kept Rice in check virtually from start to finish. That despite Rice finishing with decent statistics: 11 receptions for 117 yards, though four of his catches came in the final 3¹/₂ minutes.

The planning started immediately after the Packers defeated Atlanta in a wild-card playoff game last week, when Shurmur asked Holmgren and Lewis to spend

an hour with him early in the week to go over the 49ers' personnel. Holmgren was an assistant with the 49ers from 1986 through '91, and Lewis was with them from 1983 through '91.

Shurmur also has coached against the 49ers probably more than any defensive coordinator in the league. He faced them twice a year when he was with the Los Angeles Rams from 1982-90, including

Favre's Play Moves Him Up List

By Eric Goska

Green Bay Press-Gazette

Brett Favre is one of the top four quarterbacks in N.F.L. history based on his play in the regular season. Saturday, he became the fifth-ranked quarterback in post-season history.

With his 99.5 passer rating this season, Favre joined the likes of Steve Young and Joe Montana atop the N.F.L.'s all-time passer list. Players are ranked based on a formula that takes into account completion percentage, touchdown and interception percentages, and yards gained per attempt. Favre ranks fourth on that list behind Young, Montana and Dan Marino.

Favre began 1995 ranked 10th on the list.

Young, Montana and Marino all have played in the Super Bowl.

Though Favre has yet to reach that game, he has played like a champion in each of the last two playoff games. In fact, his performance in the Packers' 27-17 conquest of the 49ers Saturday elevated him to fifth place on the N.F.L.'s list of all-time postseason passers.

In the last two weeks, Favre has completed 45 passes in 63 attempts for 498 yards and five touchdowns. He has thrown no interceptions in that span.

As a result, Favre finds himself behind only Bart Starr, Troy Aikman, Montana and Ken Anderson in the league's list of top-rated playoff quarterbacks. Favre has played in six playoff games and his rating stands at 92.4.

The Packers' defense also aided Favre's cause. Prior to Saturday's matchup, Young was third on the postseason list with a rating of 99.5. But after having to deal with the likes of Reggie White, Sean Jones, Wayne Simmons and a host of others, Young dropped out of the top five as his rating fell to 89.4.

With a good showing in the N.F.C. Championship game next week, Favre could move past Anderson and Montana into third place. But more importantly, a strong outing by this hard-charging gunslinger might just get the Packers into the Super Bowl this year.

the final eight years as defensive coordinator. He also coached against them in each of his three seasons as defensive coordinator with the Cardinals (1991-93).

"You have to give all the credit to Fritz," cornerback Doug Evans said. "He had a hell of a game plan."

The Packers weren't eager to reveal the specifics of their plan because they expect to face the 49ers again in future playoff games. But it was clear they wanted to play as physically as possible against Rice, jamming him at the line of scrimmage with either Newsome or Evans, and then keeping as much contact with him as possible until the play finished. They managed to do that without getting called for one penalty.

The tried to confuse him by changing up their defensive alignments almost every down. Sometimes they played four defensive linemen and two linebackers; or three defensive linemen and three linebackers; or four defensive linemen and one linebacker; or their base defense.

Shurmur said he sat down late Friday night and scripted his mix of defenses, and generally stuck to it Saturday regardless of the down. It's the first time he had made such a list since he last faced the 49ers, in 1993 with the Cardinals.

"We tried to keep rolling that and hope they couldn't get a fix on us," Shurmur said. "We were just trying to reduce predictability."

The defense also made the play of the game, in the first quarter. It came after the Packers suffered a potentially demoralizing blow when they drove 48 yards on the game's first possession only to have Tim McDonald go around Darius Holland untouched and block Chris Jacke's 44-yard field goal try.

But on the 49ers' first offensive play, Wayne Simmons caused fullback Adam Walker to fumble after he caught a swing pass, and Newsome picked it up and ran 31 yards for a touchdown that stunned the 49ers.

"That was a huge play," Evans said. "We wanted to get the crowd out of it early."

Favre, meanwhile, had one of the best games of his m.v.p. season. He completed 21 of 28 passes for 299 yards, and threw two touchdown passes without an interception.

When the 49ers blitzed early, he made them pay with some big play completions. Robert Brooks (103 yards) and Keith Jackson (101) both topped the 100-yard mark in receiving despite catching only four passes each.

"(Favre) played like an m.v.p.," tight end Mark Chmura said. "We've said all along, if we're going to win it all he's going to show us the way, and he's

John Jurkovic (64) and Matt LaBounty celebrate after halting a 49ers' advance.

Brett Favre completed 21 of 28 passes for 299 yards and 2 TD's.

showing us the way."

Favre ran the offense to perfection, especially early, when he took the Packers to the blocked field goal and back-to-back touchdowns on their first three possessions. He audibled and hit Brooks on a 20-yard lob pass to set up the first touchdown after Newsome's and hit Jackson wide open over the middle for a 35-yard gain to set up the next score, which gave the Packers a 21-0 lead.

It was an overall performance that left this team thinking there are no limits to what it can accomplish. Lewis said it reminded him of the 49ers' first Super Bowl winner in '81, which featured third-year receiver Dwight Clark.

Holmgren's Return Can't Be Beat

By Tony Walter

Green Bay Press-Gazette

Mike Holmgren walked into 3Com Park Saturday morning and headed straight for the locker room. The wrong one.

"Obviously, I was daydreaming," said Holmgren, who spent several years as a 49ers assistant coach before being hired by the Packers.

"But this is a dream come true. My first game as a 49ers coach, stepping on the field after going to high school here and teaching high school, was very special."

But nothing he did then topped what he has done now, taking his own team to the conference finals with a victory over the 49ers.

"When I was coaching at Sacred Heart, we beat Piedmont Hills after we had lost 22 in a row," said Holmgren. "That was pretty big. But this, in my tenure at Green Bay, is my biggest win."

Holmgren tried to downplay his role in helping the defense plan for the 49ers offense, but he said he spent more time than usual with his defensive coaches last week.

"My big coaching point with the defense was, 'Let's watch Jerry Rice,' " said Holmgren. "Fritz (Shurmur) said, 'Is that all?' "

But it was obvious that stopping Rice was a key factory in the Packers' plan, and Holmgren paid tribute to his defense and coaches.

"We had to do a great job," he said.

"And the key to the total plan was turnovers. So we got ahead and held on for dear life."

Holmgren said the week leading up to the game was an emotional one for him, "and I knew I had to play a football game to boot," said Holmgren. "To come back and play before family and friends was something special."

The scene on the field immediately following the game was surreal.

Holmgren went to the center of the field to shake hands with 49ers coach George Seifert, then took almost 15 minutes to work his way through hordes of photographers, TV cameramen and reporters to the Packers locker room.

Along the way, he occasionally was stopped by an old acquaintance from his San Francisco days. And he found old friends up in the stands waving to him.

He had come home a winner. And he left the same way.

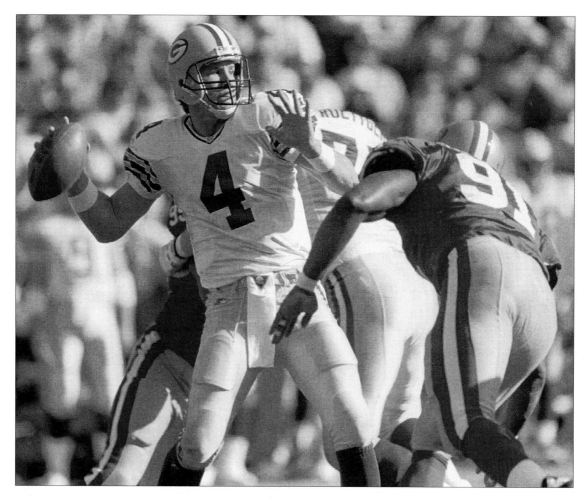

Brett Favre searches for an open receiver in the 49ers' secondary.

Victory Another Holmgren Family Affair

By Sharon Raboin

Green Bay Press-Gazette

When the game was over Sunday, Packers coach Mike Holmgren raised his head and searched the luxury boxes behind the bench.

Holmgren located his wife Kathy and their four daughters.

He waved to them; like he does before every game at Lambeau Field.

"He gives us the high sign," Kathy said. "We have to do it. That's a superstition."

But there was a problem. Many of the fans thought that Holmgren was waving to them.

Thousands of fans started cheering and waving back.

Now what?

Holmgren decided it would be appropriate to acknowledge the fans. He smiled and pumped his arms in the air while walking close to the stands with a large escort of security workers and television crews.

"I don't know," Holmgren said. "I just wanted to do that. I wanted to thank the fans. If they could have heard me, I would have yelled to them, but I couldn't. So I thanked them the only way I could."

Kathy Holmgren and their four daughters headed to the Packers administration building where Holmgren was scheduled to hold his postgame press conference.

The room was overflowing with more than 100 members of the media.

Holmgren entered the room and nodded to his family standing off to the side. Kathy was there with twins Calla and Jenny, 22; Emily, 18; and Gretchen, 14.

His daughters seldom miss a postgame press conference.

One of the first questions posed to Holmgren was about returning home to play the San Francisco 49ers in the second round of the playoffs.

"It's exciting for a couple reasons," Holmgren said. "One, we haven't played them since I came here. They're an outstanding football team so it's a great challenge. Most of our family still lives in the Bay area so I'll get to see them."

Before coming to the Packers in 1992, Holmgren worked six years with the 49ers — the first three as the quarterbacks coach and the last three as the offensive coordinator.

Holmgren was born in San Francisco. His parents were born there. He attended high school there, and was voted into the Lincoln High School Hall of Fame. Most of his family and friends live there. He is the part-owner of two restaurants, the Buchanan Grill and the Washington Square Grill,

there. He owns a home in the area.

It will be a homecoming.

But Kathy and the children probably will remain in Green Bay.

"I don't want to go," Kathy said. "It's just too emotional. I've sort of been dreading this since he took another job."

Emily, though, was trying to make a case to go.

In San Francisco, Holmgren will be spending most of his time with game preparation.

No visiting favorite restaurants. No social visits. No sightseeing.

Said Kathy: "It's a business trip. He will not leave the hotel."

And if old friends want to drop in?

"Oh no," Kathy said. "We would discourage it. He's just got too much on his mind."

In the press conference, Holmgren answered the questions with ease. He injected humor in some of his responses, drawing laughs out of the media and his children.

Kathy said her husband has the background to be center stage.

"He wanted to be a movie actor," Kathy said. "That's why he went to U.S.C. He thought he could parlay that into a film career. He was a fraternity brother with Tom Selleck."

When it was over, Holmgren walked out with his family. He stood in the hallway, giving each of them a kiss.

Later, when his business was finished, Holmgren and his family would go out to dinner. They would have the rest of the day to celebrate before turning their attention to the 49ers.

Ringing in the New Year? Holmgren was not expected to last until midnight.

"He hasn't done that since he was about 23," Kathy said. "He's not a late guy, unless he's watching a good movie.'

One Giant Leap For Packers

By Chris Havel

Green Bay Press-Gazette

Mike Holmgren visits with 49ers' coach George Seifert after the game.

This wasn't merely a step.

This was Carl Lewis soaring to a world record. This was Neil Armstrong crater-hopping on the far side of the moon. This was a leap of epic proportions. The kind that likely will be pointed to in coming years as The Turning Point in a once-proud, still-proud organization.

The Green Bay Packers are one win away from the Super Bowl.

"That hasn't hit me," general manager Ron Wolf said with a grin. "Not now."

The Packers' 27-17 victory over the San Francisco 49ers in Saturday's N.F.C. divisional playoff game defies description. It renders adjectives useless.

It does not, however, defy logic.

To knock off the defending Super Bowl champion 49ers, the Packers had to play like champions. And they did. From Craig Newsome's 31-yard fumble return for a touchdown to his diving interception with nine seconds to play, the Packers took it to the 49ers at The Stick.

And beat them with a stick.

George Koonce was asked when he knew the 49ers were in trouble.

"On Monday," the Packers' linebacker said. "When they made a big to-do about what Coach (Mike) Holmgren said about us winning it. What's he supposed to say? They tried to stir up something out of nothing. That told me one thing: They were scared."

The 49ers played like it, and for good reason.

Steve Young's wondrous legs couldn't save the 49ers' day, but they likely saved his life. The 49ers' quarterback took a beating usually reserved for washed-up boxers. He ran for 77 yards. It must have seemed like 77 years. He threw a whopping 65 passes and was sacked three times.

"There were times when he took shots that would have made a lesser quarterback lay down and quit," defensive end Sean Jones said.

Said safety LeRoy Butler: "(Young) had dirt in his eyes. His jersey was drenched. That's something he's never seen before."

"He took a beating," added linebacker Wayne Simmons. "He got out of the pocket and did some great things, but in the end, we got to him."

The Packers' knockout punch came when John Jurkovic sacked Young and forced a fumble, which Darius Holland recovered with 11:32 to play. It set the Packers up at the 49ers 38. Ten plays and four minutes later, Chris Jacke's 26-yard field goal made it 27-10.

Farewell to the kings.

The 49ers, clearly frustrated, were reduced to desperate measures. At one point, 49ers' center Bart Oates pulled off Holland's helmet and tossed it 20 yards downfield. It would be a bush move for a Pop Warner player, let alone a member of the defending Super Bowl champion.

"That's just frustration," Butler said. "You're on a glamour team. On your way to make movies and all that. Ain't no way little small-town Green Bay is supposed to come in here and kick your tail. I'd throw my helmet, too. Just like I told them, 'It sucks, doesn't it?' "

While the Packers' defense was stifling, the offense was cool as a breeze off the bay.

Brett Favre & Co. were in command from start to finish. The Packers didn't go three plays and out until the fourth quarter.

Favre was near-perfect. He completed 15 of his first 17 passes for 222 yards and a touchdown. He finished with 299 yards and two touchdowns. He com-

pleted passes to seven different receivers. He extended a seven-point lead to 21 in the blink of an eye."

"From then on," offensive coordinator Sherman Lewis said, "that clock was slower than hell. It couldn't move quick enough. The 49ers have so much firepower, so many weapons, you never really got comfortable until the end."

The Packers weren't without their own weapons.

There was Favre. Perhaps his greatest play of the game came late in the third quarter when he slipped, got up and hit Keith Jackson for a 28-yard gain.

Explained Favre with a wink, "I guess I was just showing my athleticism."

The N.F.L.'s m.v.p. stayed cool from start to finish. After the game in the locker room, he was greeted by Wolf just as he came out of the shower. While they exchanged a heartfelt handshake, Favre smiled and said, "Ron, I'd hug you, but I'm naked."

That was Favre. A cool cookie from start to finish.

Afterward, the Packers couldn't wait to get home and share this one with their fans.

"I hope the airport is still in one piece," Koonce said. "The fans back in Green Bay might tear it apart. This is great. It wasn't a fluke, either. We beat them fair and square."

"This is the best in the 25 years that I've been here," Packers president Bob Harlan said. "The job Mike and Ron have done since they've come here is, well, it's magnificent."

Afterward, a smiling but soaked Mike Holmgren accepted compliments in his usual modest style. Any pride that swelled in his chest was well-deserved. Already, though, he was looking ahead to Dallas or a home game at Lambeau Field.

Asked if it all had sunk in yet, Holmgren replied, "You know, a lot of things haven't sunk in yet. I'll probably get on that plane and tears will start flowing out of my eyes. It was a special week."

Dream Dies In Dallas

Packers Again Fall Short in Super Bowl Quest

By Pete Dougherty

Green Bay Press-Gazette

IRVING, Tex., Jan. 14, 1996 — The Packers' quest to become one of the N.F.L.'s premier teams stopped Sunday as it has for three straight years now: On a January day in Texas Stadium.

What made their 38-27 loss to the Cowboys different this time was that it came in the N.F.C. Championship game instead of the divisional playoffs of the last two years, and in a game that was highly competitive.

After losing to the Cowboys by a combined score of of 62-26 in the 1994 and '95 playoffs, the Packers this time played well enough to take a 27-24 lead into the fourth quarter.

The Cowboys still managed to prove they have an important edge on the Packers, namely a running back (Emmitt Smith) and an offensive line that again took over with the game on the line in the fourth quarter. But the Packers still were within one play of the lead in the fourth quarter until quarterback Brett Favre was intercepted at the Dallas 20 with 9:59 to play. Green Bay left Texas Stadium feeling like it had taken its biggest step yet in trying to become one of the N.F.L.'s genuine championship contenders.

In fact, the Packers were saying they are only a home-field advantage away from defeating their long-time rival, the Dallas Cowboys.

"I think we've closed the gap considerably," said Ron Wolf, the Packers' general manager. "But again, our team isn't structured to run around on this (artificial turf), and I don't think we can afford to structure it that way."

So the Cowboys move on to the Super Bowl in two weeks against Pittsburgh, while the Packers finish the season 13-6 overall and one game short of their first trip to the Super Bowl since January 1968. They had one of the N.F.L.'s most consistently effective offenses led by the 26-year-old Favre, and a defense that had played its best football in the playoffs until it finally buckled in the second half against the Cowboys.

When asked what his priorities will be for off-season personnel moves, Wolf said, "Shore up the defense and add something offensively again, something the other team has to worry about a little bit."

The difference Sunday was the Packers' inability to stop Smith with the game on the line and Favre's somewhat uneven play on a day when he needed to be nearly perfect for the Packers to win.

Smith gained 50 of his 150 yards in the fourth quarter and was a key in the Cowboys' most important possession of the day, an efficient 90-yard touchdown drive that started late in the third quarter with the Packers leading, 27-24. He gained 27 yards on five carries, and Dallas held the ball for

Dallas' Michael Irvin outjumps Packers cornerback Craig Newsome (21) for the ball.

Edgar Bennett rambles for big yardage against the Dallas defense.

seven minutes 19 seconds in a drive reminiscent of its five more dominating victories over the Packers in the last three years. When Smith scored on a five-yard run with 12:24 to play, the Cowboys were back in the lead at 31-27.

Favre, though, had the Packers driving when he threw the interception that would prove fatal to their season. On first down from Dallas' 46, he rolled slightly to his right, looking for either of his two tight ends, Keith Jackson or Mark Chmura. He didn't think either was open, so he continued loping to his right and made the type of scrambling throw that had helped win him the N.F.L.'s m.v.p. this year. He tried to hit receiver Mark Ingram about 30 yards downfield along the sidelines, but Ingram didn't come back to the ball like he had expected, and cornerback Larry Brown stepped in for the interception at about the 20.

"It was a scramble situation, and I don't think he and Mark were on the same page for the improvisation," said Steve Mariucci, the Packers' quarterbacks coach. "He's made a lot big plays on the run and out of the pocket."

Two plays later — a 36-yard pass that receiver Michael Irvin caught after it bounced off cornerback Doug Evans' back, and a 16-yard touchdown run by Smith — and the Cowboys were comfortably ahead, 38-27.

"It was three minutes like an avalanche," safety LeRoy Butler said. "We were ahead, and the next thing I knew we're down by 11 and they can utilize what they do best, run the ball."

Up to that point, the Packers had done a decent job of slowing Aikman, Irvin and Smith. As he did last week at San Francisco, Packers defensive coordinator Fritz Shurmur mixed the Packers' defensive fronts, regularly using his base defense, a nickel alignment that sometimes had Butler near the line of scrimmage, and his three-linemen, three-linebacker set that had proved so valuable throughout the play-offs.

In their other recent meetings, the Cowboys had demoralized the Packers with several big plays a game, but Sunday their longest gain was Irvin's 36-yard reception.

Smith, meanwhile, had 100 yards after three quarters, but he needed 27 carries to do it, which is an average of only 3.7 yards a carry.

And one of the Cowboys' first-half touchdowns came on a short field after defensive tackle Leon Lett read a screen pass and stepped in front of fullback Dorsey Levens for an interception that gave them the ball at the Packers' 13.

"Their big play ability today we got under control," Shurmur said. "We don't like the score, but we like some of the things in this game that were different (from the previous five games against Dallas)."

What remained the same was Dallas taking over in the fourth quarter. The Cowboys were helped by a huge edge in time of possession — they had the ball 38:56 to the Packers' 21:04 by game's end — and by the fourth quarter, Smith and an offensive line that averages 321 pounds per man appeared to wear down the Packers.

Shurmur had tried to keep his defensive line as fresh as possible by rotating all eight linemen he had suited up for the game, but nose tackle John Jurkovic's game-ending knee injury late in the first half cut into that rotation.

"You have to give them credit," Packers linebacker George Koonce said. "They ran the ball down our throat in the third and fourth quarter."

Favre wasn't sharp early, throwing incompletions on his first five passes and having his sixth intercepted by Lett. By early in the second quarter, he was only 2-for-8, but both completions were touchdowns. A 73-yarder to Brooks, who had blown past Brown at the line of scrimmage on a slant and then

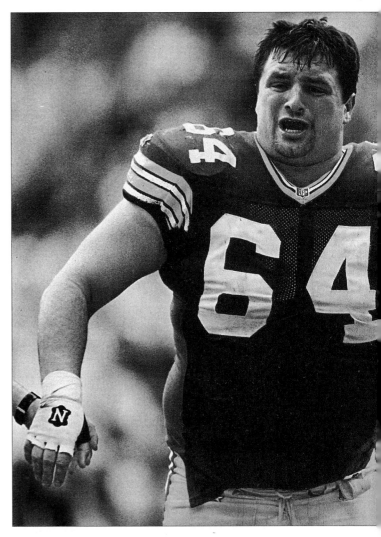

John Jurkovic was forced to leave the game early due to a knee injury.

outran the rest of the secondary to score untouched; and a 24-yarder down the middle of the field to Jackson.

So despite the slow start, the Packers led, 17-14, barely more than one-fourth of the way through the game.

"He played through (the early-game jitters)," Mariucci said.

Favre finished the day 21-for-39 for 307 yards and three touchdowns. But Brown's fourth-quarter interception at Dallas' 20 was more than the Packers could withstand, because the defense couldn't keep Smith out of the end zone.

"It's tough to lose like this. We did have an opportunity to win," tight end Mark Chmura said. "But this was much different than the first five games (against Dallas). When they mention the (premier) teams in the N.F.C., we should be on that list. We're a pretty damn good football team."

A Tough Loss, But Surely No Shame

By Chris Havel
Green Bay Press-Gazette

Drama. Anger. Ecstasy. Outrage.
Green Bay's 38-27 loss to the Dallas Cowboys in Sunday's N.F.C. Championship game at Texas Stadium had everything. Everything, that is, except a happy ending for the Packers.

The Cowboys, showing that good guys don't always wear white, proved to be cheapshot artists and thugs. They also proved to be too much for the Packers on their own turf.

Too much Emmitt Smith. Too much Michael Irvin. Too much Leon Lett.

Same names. Same game. It's a tired refrain. This is Stephen King's version of Groundhog Day. The alarm goes off and it's one nightmarish episode after another.

"We were shooting at 'em and shooting at 'em," said LeRoy Butler, "but we just couldn't come up with enough plays to win."

The Packers took their final shot trailing, 31-27, with 10 minutes to play, Brett Favre rolled right and steered a pass toward Mark Ingram, but the Cowboys' Larry Brown picked it off. Two plays later, Smith scored and it was all over but the shouting.

"Brett was trying to improvise and make something happen," said Packers quarterbacks coach Steve Mariucci. "You win some. You lose some. That was one for the defense."

Favre had better days. He was 21 of 39 for 307 yards and three touchdowns, but his two intercep-

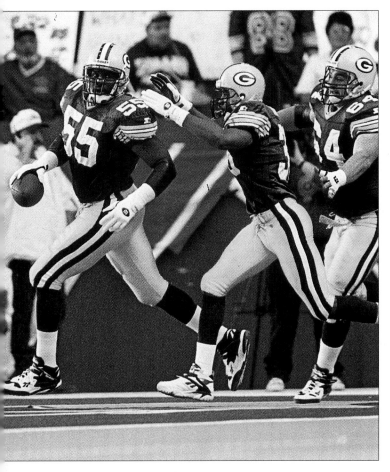

Fred Strickland's fumble return for a TD was called back due to a penalty.

tions were costly. But Favre didn't lose this game. He merely failed to win it.

"Brett didn't play like he has been, but he still put us in a position to win it," said Sean Jones.

"Twenty-seven points," added Butler, "should be enough to win." .

At Lambeau Field, it probably is. The Packers lost this game as much because of pitfalls against St. Louis and Tampa Bay as they did because of anything that occurred Sunday.

Nevertheless, this was a terrific game played the

way God and Lombardi intended. Tough. Hardnosed. Physical. Championship football. Great stuff. Begrudgingly, and with the tenacity of a bare-knuckles brawler, the Packer finally bowed.

That someone had to lose offered no consolation.

"One week you're euphoric," said Packers general manager Ron Wolf. "The next week you feel like a piece of slime on the bottom of the ocean. That's exactly what I feel like."

No wonder. Wrestle with pigs and you get dirty.

The Cowboys' Erik Williams is the dirtiest of them all. His chop block that crushed John Jurkovic's left knee was a crime. Williams ought to have a bail bondsman, not an agent.

"You play long enough in football, things tend to even out," said Jurkovic. "So maybe one day Williams will get his."

Today, the Cowboys star is tarnished.

The Packers, however, should hold their heads up high.

They battled back from a 14-3 deficit to take leads of 17-14 and 27-24. They gave as much as they got. They went facemask to facemask with the N.F.L.'s best team and didn't blink.

"The Cowboys should be proud of the way they stood up to us," said Jones. "We're the more physical team."

Added Mark Chmura, "We'll knock your block off. There ain't no finesse on this team."

No quit, either.

"Until the last play, you keep fighting," said Mariucci. "And every man likes a good fight."

Indeed, the Packers fought the good fight. It's just that Coach Mike Holmgren's brain was no match for Emmitt Smith's legs. He racked up 150 yards in 35 carries. He was the difference.

"This team," promised Reggie White, "will win a championship."

Believe it.

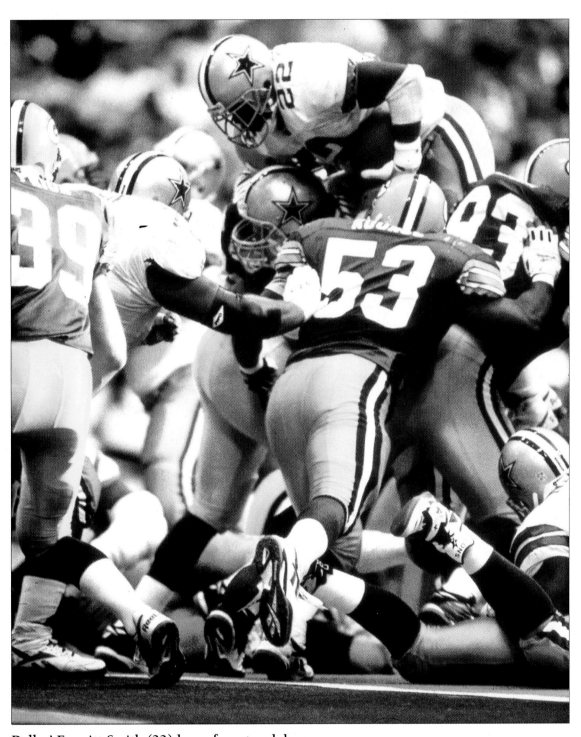

Dallas' Emmitt Smith (22) leaps for a touchdown.

Prime Time Pounding

Pack Whips Eagles, 39-13, in Monday Night Thriller

By Pete Dougherty

Green Bay Press-Gazette

GREEN BAY — Brett Favre opened Monday night's showdown with the Philadelphia Eagles by misfiring on his first five passes and taking the

Packers a total of nine yards the first three times they had the ball.

They had run so few plays that by possession No. 4 they still were on Coach Mike Holmgren's first-15-plays script, and next up, by chance was a call that's been Holmgren's most reliable since bringing his version of the San Francisco 49ers' offense to Green Bay in 1992: A screen pass.

Favre goaded the Eagles' heavy rush, then dumped the ball to halfback Edgar Bennett, who picked up 11 yards and a first down. As unremarkable as it appeared at the time, it became the catalyst for an offensive explosion that saw the Packers' remarkably diverse offense embarrass the Eagles, 39-13, in front of a national TV audience and a jubilant record crowd at Lambeau Field of 60,666 spectators.

After the game, Holmgren characterized his script's screen call as "timely."

"Sometimes it's just a matter of throwing a screen pass, getting a completion or calming things down a lit-

tle bit," he said. "I think that's what happened tonight."

The win puts the Packers at 2-0 with a combined scoring differential of 73-16.

The startling part of Monday night's blowout was the quality of opponent. If last week's season-opening 34-3 hammering of Tampa Bay could be written off as catching a weak team in its first game with a new coach, Monday night by all appearances was to present a real challenge.

The Eagles came in as one of the N.F.L.'s teams on the rise and regarded as a genuine contender for the N.F.C. Eastern Division title.

They also had a coach, Ray Rhodes, who has a reputation as a master motivator, not to mention an intimate knowledge of the Packers after serving as Holmgren's defensive coordinator in 1992 and '93.

But the game was over by halftime, when Green Bay led, 30-7, and it is sure to open eyes around the N.F.L. After Monday night, the question that has dogged the Packers for the past three years — whether they've closed the gap on Dallas and San Francisco — seems to have disappeared.

"What I saw tonight was a team that realized it can be a great team," said Sean Jones, a Packers defensive end.

And it all started with the screen pass to Bennett.

Holmgren has leaned heavily on that play in his five years as coach, especially when his offense was less talented than now, and often when it was strug-

Brett Favre flees as Eagles linebacker James Willis chases him from the pocket.

gling to move the ball any other way.

It's become such an effective weapon that last season Chicago Bears coach Dave Wannstedt showed his team an entire videotape of Packers' screens the week before their second meeting.

Bennett still managed to score on screens of 17 and 16 yards that day, and on Monday night he did it again. Besides getting that first catch, he also put on the finishing touch in the third quarter, taking a screen pass 25 yards for the Packers' final touchdown and a 37-7 lead.

"It's something we practice and Mike harps on more than anything in this offense," tight end Mark Chmura said. "You don't see many teams run it in the red zone (i.e., inside the opponent's 20), and we run it down there real well. We pride ourselves on it."

The first completion probably did more than just get Favre started. It might have taken the edge off pass-rushing defensive ends William Fuller and Mike Mamula.

After that 11-yard screen, Favre completed 13 of his next 20 passes while taking the Packers to five straight scores — three touchdowns and two field goals — before the half ended.

"With their pursuit, the way to slow it down is with draws and screens," Favre said.

Keith Jackson (88) highsteps a Philadelphia tackler.

Then the Packers' offensive diversity overwhelmed the Eagles.

The Eagles kept Jackson and Chmura from getting behind the secondary and held them to four receptions for 58 yards.

But when Philadelphia's big cornerbacks, Bobby Taylor (6-3, 216 pounds) and Troy Vincent (6-0, 194), tried to jam wide receivers Robert Brooks and Antonio Freeman at the line of scrimmage, they had little help from the safeties. The price was devastating.

Brooks gashed them for 130 yards on five receptions, a 26-yard average per catch.

After catching a 25-yard pass on a double move for the Packers' first touchdown, he streaked straight past tight one-on-one coverage for three big plays on perfect throws from Favre: A 38-yarder behind Vincent that set up a touchdown; a 33-yarder behind safety Eric Zomalt that set up a field goal;

and a 20-yarder behind Vincent for the final first-half touchdown.

With weapons such as Brooks, Freeman, Chmura, Jackson and Bennett, Holmgren kept the Eagles off balance with a variety of formations — two tight ends on some plays, three or four receivers on others, and the standard two-back set on still others.

Once Favre got started, they all dominated completely, gaining 432 total yards, averaging 15.4 yards a completion, and rushing for more yards (171) than any game last season.

"This guy right here," said Jones, pointing at Favre's locker, "just does some things that aren't coached. It's God-given. That ball he threw to Brooks on the second (20-yard) touchdown: The ball on a line, on the money, effortlessly. The kind of confidence, where does it come from?"

Execution Makes the Difference

By John Morton

Green Bay Press-Gazette

So much for the similarities.

While the schemes and formations and other X's and O's may have been common for the Packers and Eagles Monday night, when it came down to execution the two teams looked nothing alike.

The Packers executed. The Eagles got executed.

"For as much pressure that was built up for this game ... let's face it, we're pretty good," said Packers safety LeRoy Butler. "There's no sugar-coating it."

While the offense has shined for the Packers in the early going, the defense has shared the spotlight at least as much. And the defensive effort has been equally as flashy. When the first half ended Monday, the Green Bay defense already owned 10 takeaways — having added four against the Eagles. Last year, it was Week 10 when it reached that total.

Repeating the start it had against Tampa Bay, the defense caused two Philadelphia turnovers Monday in the opening quarter. Again, the takeaways led to the offense's first two scores.

Despite the highly anticipated arrival of turnovers this year, the Packers' defense has hardly relied upon them. Instead, it's come down to speed and solid tackling.

"It ain't no magic trick," said defensive tackle Gilbert Brown. "It's very fundamental."

And it's consistency. In the opener, the Packer defense held the Buccaneers to a paltry 59 rushing yards. Against the Eagles, it allowed just 59 more.

When Philadelphia running back Ricky Watters can't run, he usually catches passes out in the flat to make up for it. On Monday, he caught one pass for one yard.

"He (Watters) can normally make that first guy miss," said Packers linebacker George Koonce, who shared the team lead with five tackles and added an interception. "We needed good, crisp tackling."

Still, some Packers found the Eagles' formations to their liking.

"It's a typical, San Francisco-style, West Coast offense," said defensive tackle Santana Dotson. "We see that every day (in practice)."

Twice Dotson got to Eagles quarterback Rodney Peete for sacks, including the first hit in the end zone in which defensive end Reggie White finished off for a fourth-quarter safety. Dotson also tipped the pass that Koonce picked off.

"Their front four is as good as there is around," Peete said.

"They've got Reggie (White) and (defensive end) Sean Jones with the power, and Santana (Dotson) with speed," he said. "And they've got some linebackers that can run."

Added Eagles coach Ray Rhodes, "They've got speed."

There was, however, a pass-catch and lateral between Philadelphia receivers Chris T. Jones and Irving Fryar that went for 62 yards in the second quarter, setting up an Eagles touchdown.

Then there was the last-minute drive by ex-Packer Ty Detmer against a prevent defense for the Eagles' second touchdown.

Hardly stuff to get upset about.

Nonetheless, a straight-faced Butler said: "We could have played a little bit better."

White was serious about things as well, knowing something special was within reach.

"We need to keep playing like this," he said. "We may not have this opportunity again."

Mike Johnson (56) keys in on Eagles halfback Charlie Garner as he turns the corner.

This One Was Over Shortly After Coin Toss

By Chris Havel

Green Bay Press-Gazette

One could sift through the Eagles' wreckage for clues as to why the Packers annihilated coach Ray Rhodes' outfit. Or one could merely point a tape recorder at noted philosopher/nose tackle Gilbert Brown.

"Ain't no secrets. Ain't no tricks," he said. "We just played good football."

Brown, a big man of few words, was correct in both his analysis of the Packers' 39-13 shelling of Philadelphia and his decision not to overstate the obvious.

Simply put, the Packers are one of the N.F.L.'s top teams. The Eagles are not. That debate started to die in the split-second between Chris T. Jones' catch and Doug Evan's interception, all of which happened on the Eagles' first play.

Evan's sleight of hand not only set the tone but the tint, the hue and the color of the Packers' first home appearance on Monday night football in a decade. This game was green and gold and red (with Eagles' embarrassment) all over.

The Packers are unbeatable and untested and an improvement on the '95 team. The defense steals and the running game lives. The Packers have given all the Tuesday Morning Quarterbacks little to nit-pick.

OK. So Eugene Robinson misplayed the catch-and-lateral. And George Koonce and Sean Jones dropped would-be interceptions. And Mike Arthur's snap sailed higher than Hakeem Olajuwon can reach with a fish net.

In the past, those would've been headlines. Today, they're footnotes.

The Packers have won 19 of their last 20 at Lambeau Field, a feat unmatched even by Lombardi's teams. This is a franchise whose present has finally outrun its past, fueled by a team whose future seems limitless.

The Packers came in as 8-point favorites for a reason. The reason is no one in their right mind would bet on the Eagles unless they were getting two scores before the pregame introductions. The Packers are hot. Or as an acquaintance noted, "If this were college football, the Packers would be No. 1."

By that logic, if this were college football, the Packers would be hosting the TCU Horned Frogs instead of the San Diego Chargers this weekend. Of course, the Horned Frogs are not the Chargers, but then the Eagles weren't the Eagles. They were the Buccaneers in midnight green.

The Packers took the zip out of the Eagles by forcing three turnovers on their first four possessions. Asked if his presence as honorary game captain affected the outcome, ex-Packers center Larry McCarren laughed and said, "Oh, I figured that and Ed West losing the coin toss pretty much sealed it."

Yep. This one was over early.

In the span of two quarters, the Packers cut the Eagles in half, reducing a Super Bowl XXXI contender to a .500 team with a quarterback controversy.

This is how tough it was on the Eagles: Their only break came on the bad snap that caused the Packers to botch a field-goal try. Their reward was the ball at their own 3-yard line. That series ended with Reggie White and Santan Dotson sacking Rodney Peete for a safety.

Talk about costly turnovers.

Ty Detmer once more was the second-best quarterback at Lambeau Field, right behind Brett Favre but well ahead of Peete — whose poor decisions were rivaled only by his poor throws.

Fullback William Henderson celebrates his second quarter TD.

Pack Routs Chargers

Defense Dominates, Boosts Record to 3-0

By Pete Dougherty

Green Bay Press-Gazette

GREEN BAY — And so it goes, as it has for three weeks with the Green Bay Packers' defense:

It holds an opponent to fewer than two touchdowns, and two defensive linemen have big games — in this case, Sean Jones and Reggie White with two sacks each.

Then, tackle Santana Dotson draws a huge postgame crowd of reporters because as a key new player this year he surely must be a reason why the Packers are holding opponents to 192 yards a game.

And then there's Gilbert Brown. The stat sheet after the Packers' 42-10 blowout of San Diego on Sunday says he had one assisted tackle for the day, and nothing more. But that can't begin to measure what this massive, 350-pound tackle brings to the heart of this defense.

"Gilbert gets all the dirty work," Jones said. "We let Gilbert sit in there and pick up all the trash, and Reggie and I get to slash and go. That's his fault for being so good. Without a guy like that (for the offense) to respect — that's what makes everything go."

For a third straight week the Packers' defense was as dominating as their offense — their average margin of victory in their 3-0 start is 38-9.

And it all starts with the defensive line of Jones, White, Dotson and Brown.

White, at age 34, still is the key and remains one of the most dominating players in the game. He had several pressures to go along with his two sacks, one of which caused a fumble that the Chargers recovered.

"(The Packers) took Reggie White as a cornerstone, like a Michael Jordan, and added guys around him," linebacker George Koonce said.

Brown, a fourth-year pro, quietly has become as valued a piece as any of his highly paid linemates, who are under contract for a combined average salary of $8.4 million a year.

Facing an offensive line that Bobby Ross calls his best in five years as the Chargers' coach, the Packers shut down a San Diego rushing game that was averaging 100 yards a game with three very different runners splitting time in its one-back attack: 240-pound Leonard Russell, 218-pound Aaron Hayden and 196-pound Terrell Fletcher.

The Packers held them to a combined 33 yards and a 2.5-yard average per carry. Brown is not the only reason, but he is their primary run stopper in the middle of the field.

With that under control, the Packers besieged quarterback Stan Humphries. Besides sacking him four times they had several other hard hits and had him scrambling most of the day. He finished with barely over a 50 percent completion percentage (16-

Linebacker Eugene Robinson (41) and Brian Williams (51) pile up a San Diego receiver.

for-30) and only 130 yards passing.

As they have all year, the Chargers generally kept in a tight end on pass plays, which gave them six blockers against four linemen and an occasional blitz from linebacker Wayne Simmons or safety LeRoy Butler. But which two should they have double-teamed?

"(Most weeks) you consider which guy is the pass-rush specialist and you try to eliminate him," Humphries said. "It's kind of hard to do when you've got four guys up there."

Brown, the only Packers' starter on the defensive line who doesn't have a sack this season, drew as many double teams as anyone.

"Big Gil, you have to get him double teamed or some offensive lineman is going to get pushed into the quarterback for sure," Koonce said.

Dotson also has been a huge factor since the Packers signed him in the offseason for an average of

$2 million a year to replace John Jurkovic in the starting lineup.

The Packers have allowed an unusually low completion percentage so far (46.5 percent), and that's where the pass rush is crucial. Fritz Shurmur, their defensive coordinator, said he's blitzed a little more this year than last, but Dotson's rushing speed from the middle of the line has been a bigger factor as more teams go to short quarterback dropbacks.

"In the 80's you had the small linebacker-types that you called defensive ends (as the key pass rushers)," Shurmur said. "Now you have to get some-body in (the quarterback's) face quick. That's the way the game has changed, and (Dotson) has been a factor in there."

The Packers started well early last season also, holding the Rams and Giants to 17 points or less in two of the first three games before hard times hit in the middle of the year. But even in those early games, they were giving up much more yardage than now — the Rams and Bears both gained more than 300 yards against Green Bay in the first three games of '95.

"Our team speed is so much better than a year ago," Jones said.

Bennett, Henderson 'Run' Up Score Behind No-Name Line

By Eric Schurer

Green Bay Press-Gazette

With a boost from a determined offensive line, a bulldozing fullback and improvement from Edgar Bennett, the Packers continue to show a surprisingly potent ground game.

With 132 rushing yards in Sunday's 42-10 win over San Diego, the Packers topped the 100-yard mark for the third straight game, the first time they've done that in Mike Holmgren's four-plus years as head coach.

Bennett ran for 65 yards on 13 carries, giving him 220 for the season with a nifty 5.1 per carry average, a vast improvement over last season's average of 3.4

Bennett is getting a lot of help, however. And not just from Dorsey Levens, who chipped in 39 yards on nine carries (4.3 average).

William Henderson, a load of a fullback at 248 pounds, is helping open up running room for Bennett. On Bennett's 10-yard touchdown run in the first quarter, Henderson paved the way by cutting down San Diego's all-pro linebacker Junior Seau with a devastating block.

Henderson's day didn't end with blocking for Bennett, either. The second-year fullback from North Carolina caught four passes for 26 yards, including his first N.F.L. touchdown, an 8-yarder from Brett Favre in the second quarter.

"It's nice to use my hands and show off other talents once in a while," said Henderson. "But my job as a fullback is to block."

He also showed good form with his celebratory leap into the stands after the score.

Success on the ground now will keep opposing defenses playing the guessing game all season, according to Adam Timmerman. "When the running game is working, it makes everything in the offense that much better," he said.

Blitzing Bolt Short-Circuited

By John Morton

Green Bay Press-Gazette

As expected, San Diego linebacker Junior Seau blitzed hard and blitzed often Sunday. And there were times he had Packers quarterback Brett Favre on the run.

Then again, Favre often does his best on the run.

Out of the 14 times Seau full-out blitzed, he only did damage on five plays. And the damage was minor. Before the game, Favre said that if his offense can pick up Seau's blitzes 50 percent of the time or more, the Packers would be safe.

"He's a great player, but the way he runs around he sometimes takes himself out of plays," Packers tackle Earl Dotson said of Seau, an All-Pro for six straight years.

Packers guard Aaron Taylor agreed.

"Junior makes a lot of plays, but he also misses a lot."

Seau over-committed himself on several successful Packers plays, especially when Green Bay ran up the middle — the spot where Seau would be if he stayed put.

Two plays stand out in particular: In the second quarter, Seau was left in the Packers' backfield as running back Edgar Bennett burst off tackle for nine yards. A similar play helped running back Dorsey Levens dash for 12 yards in the fourth quarter — right up the gut.

Bennett and Levens also were effective on picking up Seau before he could reach Favre on three different plays.

Two such blocks came in the third quarter when the Chargers blitzed Seau on nearly every defensive down. Favre hit tight end Mark Chmura for 11 yards and wide receiver Robert Brooks for eight yards.

In the second quarter, Bennett's backfield block on Seau allowed Favre to scramble for six yards and a first down.

"We did an adequate job," running back William Henderson said of the backfield's performance on limiting Seau. "He didn't alter the game."

Seau was harder on himself.

"I stunk up the field," he said.

Favre acknowledged that the blitz did make for some tense moments.

"I think they're pretty good at it," he said. "We had to get rid of the ball pretty quick."

Surprisingly, the Packers didn't manage to hit on any big plays after picking up the blitz — a scenario that leads to man-to-man coverage. Their longest play against the blitz was the 11-yard pass to Chmura.

But Seau didn't have the big play either. In fact, the Chargers' lone sack of Favre came on a play in which Seau dropped back into pass coverage.

The five plays where Seau did make a difference:

■ Seau's pressure on a first-quarter blitz caused Favre to hurry a throw to Brooks, which was intercepted by San Diego cornerback Dwayne Harper.

■ In the second quarter, Seau trapped Brooks behind the line on a reverse, leading to a seven-yard loss.

■ Also in the second quarter, he hurried Favre into a screen pass that hit Bennett in the back of the legs.

■ In the third quarter, Seau hurried and knocked Favre down for a third-down incompletion.

■ Also in the third quarter, Seau blitzed up the middle and stopped Levens at the line of scrimmage for no gain.

Dorsey Levens (25) romps off tackle for big yardage against the Chargers' defense.

Robert Brooks (87) sprints through the Chargers' empty secondary following a blitz.

Domination By Any Stat

By Eric Goska

Green Bay Press-Gazette

Call it domination. The Packers have won three straight games by more than 25 points for only the second time since joining the professional ranks in 1921. After crushing the Chargers 42-10 Sunday, Green Bay has outscored its opponents 115-26, a difference of 89 points.

Such a differential suggests the team is clicking in all phases. The statistics bear this out.

Brett Favre became the first Packers quarterback to throw 10 touchdown passes in the first three games of a season. Green Bay has given up just one touchdown pass and its opponents have managed an abysmal 26.8 pass efficiency rating.

Edgar Bennett and his cohorts have run the ball more than 30 times in three straight games, a first under Coach Mike Holmgren. Opponents have yet to gain more than 59 yards rushing in a game and are averaging fewer than three yards a carry.

The Packers are converting third downs into first downs at a rate of better than 55 percent. Their opponents, meanwhile, have cashed in at a 20.6-percent clip.

The special teams also have contributed. Desmond Howard's 118 yards in punt returns against the Chargers was the third-most ever in a game by a Packer. Craig Hentrich owns a 45.9 average on eight punts. And Chris Jacke has been successful on his last 75 extra point tries, the third-longest streak in team annals.

This all-around consistency has led to the blowouts. Not since the 1961 team defeated Baltimore, 45-7; Cleveland, 49-17, and Minnesota, 33-7, have

Quick Hits

■ The Packers are 3-0 for the first time since 1982.

■ Favre's pass efficiency rating Sunday was 89.2, ending a string of four consecutive games in which his rating had been greater than 100. Favre's rating after three games is 116.4.

■ LeRoy Butler's 90-yard interception return was the fourth-longest in team history behind those of Tim Lewis (90 yards), Rebel Steiner (94) and Hal Van Every (91). Butler has 501 yards on 25 career interceptions. Only Bobby Dillon (976), Herb Adderley (795) and Willie Wood (699) have more yards.

■ Bennett has caught at least one pass in 51 consecutive games. The only Packers to catch one or more passes during a longer span are Sterling Sharpe (103 games) and James Lofton (58).

■ Until Sunday, Bennett had not lost a fumble the last 726 times he handled the ball.

the Packers manhandled three straight opponents.

"We have a good football team, but it always surprises me in this league when there's that much point differential," said Holmgren. "I don't expect games like that. I've been in so many close games over the years that those are more the kind of games you expect to play."

Last year, the Packers' largest margin of victory was 22 points (35-13 over Tampa Bay). In Holmgren's first four years, Green Bay defeated only six opponents by more than 25 points.

Gutsy Packers Rally

Jacke Boots Winning Kick in Overtime

By Pete Dougherty

Green Bay Press-Gazette

GREEN BAY — With the game on the line, Packers coach Mike Holmgren turned to gut instinct.

There was still more than 11 minutes left in overtime Monday night when he had to decide whether kicker Chris Jacke should try the 53-yard field goal that beat the San Francisco 49ers, 23-20, and there was good reason to not risk it.

| Packers | 23 |
| 49ers | 20 |

If Jacke missed, after all, the 49ers would get a short field, starting at the spot of the kick, their own 43. That's only a couple of completions from a possible game-winning kick of their own.

In fact, faced with almost the exact same fourth-and-five decision in the first half, when far less was at stake, Holmgren had passed up the 51- or 52-yard kick. He thought about how well his defense was playing, chose not to risk the eight yards a miss would cost, and tried instead to convert a difficult fourth-and-five that failed.

But this time, early in overtime of the Packers' biggest game of the 1996 season so far, Holmgren consulted his instincts honed by 26 years coaching football in high school, college and the N.F.L. They told him to go for the kill.

"I figured, shoot, let's try it," Holmgren said.

That instinct to go for the jugular was in contrast to what 49ers coach George Seifert decided to do in the game's final minutes.

Seifert played it safe in the last two minutes of regulation when he had quarterback Elvis Grbac down the ball in the middle of the field on third down, setting up a straight-on field goal rather than taking one shot at the end zone from the 10-yard line. It was the safe play and gave the 49ers a 20-17 lead, but it also left Packers quarterback Brett Favre with 1 minute 50 seconds and needing only to get into field-goal position for the tie.

Holmgren, on the other hand, took the shot when he got the chance. Favre took the Packers to San Francisco's 13 with only 30 seconds and no timeouts remaining, and he tried three straight passes into the end zone before Jacke tied the game with a 31-yard field goal.

"I mean you get inside the 20 down there, get that close and settle for a field goal?" receiver Don Beebe said. "No way. We were trying to win the game."

Then, when it came time to make the field-goal decision in overtime, Holmgren didn't hesitate. No timeout, no deliberation. He sent Jacke and the field-goal unit onto the field almost immediately after Favre had thrown the ball away to avoid a sack on third down.

Perhaps the decision was made easier after watching his defense in perhaps its finest hour. It had held the 49ers to only 75 yards and three points

With a pair of 49ers defenders hanging on, Keith Jackson (88) rumbles for a Packers' first down.

With Reggie White (92) in pursuit, 49ers quarterback Elvis Grbac searches for open field.

in the second half, with the field goal set up by an interception at the Packers' 12.

"Mike made (the decision), and it was the right one," said Fritz Shurmur, the Packers' defensive coordinator. "Nolan (Cromwell, the special-teams coach) was comfortable with the distance, and Mike was comfortable with the distance. If (the defense) had to go back out there, we'd have to fight and find a way to knock 'em outta there."

The kick would end up doing wonders for Jacke. In the last two years, his accuracy had slipped a bit from the high standards, he had set earlier in his career: In 1994 and '95 combined, he made 73.5 percent of his field goals (36-for-49) after making 78.4 percent of his first five years.

This season, he was 7-for-10 going into Monday night, including missing a 38-yarder in the kicker-friendly conditions of the Kingdome in Seattle. And he missed an extra point last week at Chicago.

Among other things, he was stung in the Seattle game when Holmgren passed up a 52-yard field goal

in the second quarter, before Jacke had even missed a kick that day.

"A lot of people — the press and some fans — have been giving him a hard time since his misses at Tampa Bay and Seattle," said Craig Hentrich, the Packers' punter and Jacke's holder. "Maybe this will get them off his back."

Jacke went into the kick having made more than 50 percent (16-for-25) of his attempts from 50 yards or more, though he hadn't tried one from that distance this season. At 53-yards, it would tie for the second longest field goal in Packers' history, behind the 54-yarder he had hit at Detroit's Silverdome on Jan. 2, 1994.

His teammates on the field-goal unit didn't say much to him, and it helped that there was no timeout other than the stop in play. Hentrich assured him the hold would be good, and he saw a confident look when Jacke said, "Here's the spot. Let's kick it through."

"I knew it (was good) as soon as he hit it," Hentrich said. "I don't need to look up. I can tell by the sound now."

Said Jacke, "It was probably one of the better balls I've kicked in a long time."

It came on a day when Jacke kicked five field goals and became the Packers' second all-time scorer with 763 points. That surpasses Paul Hornung (760 points), with Don Hutson (823) in the lead.

The last two kicks — the 31-yarder to tie with eight seconds left and the game winner — were about as pressure-filled as field goals can get during the regular season.

This, after all, was against the N.F.L.'s premier team of the 80's and 90's, the 49ers. And it was in the national spotlight of Monday Night Football in a game that matched probably the best two teams in the league, at least the best at the seven-week mark of the season.

"He'll sleep well," Hentrich said. "That's the ultimate. And if you miss it, you want to walk to the other sideline. That's the life of a kicker."

A courageous Brett Favre completed 28 of 61 passes for 395 yards.

Favre, Reserves Deliver When It Counts

By John Morton

Green Bay Press-Gazette

Not only did Brett Favre get it done Monday night, he got it done without his starting wide receiver, running back and right tackle. And because of some big hits he took down the stretch, he got it done without all his bearings.

But when it comes to the two-minute drill, the Packers quarterback showed he can take matters into his own hands.

"He's always done well at that," Green Bay coach Mike Holmgren said of Favre, who led the Packers' last-minute march that resulted in a game-tying field goal with eight seconds left in regulation. "We practice that a lot. Now I can say, 'See why we practice that?'"

In a season filled with lopsided victories, only

Chris Jacke's 53-yard field goal in overtime gave the Packers a 23-20 win.

once has Favre been called upon to rally his team. It came in the loss at Minnesota, and it was short-lived due to a fumble. On Monday, he pulled through.

As did others. Because of injuries, Don Beebe was in for Robert Brooks, Dorsey Levens was in for Edgar Bennett and Bruce Wilkerson was in for Earl Dotson.

"A couple of years ago we didn't have the depth," Favre said of the replacements. "Some of them don't get many reps in practice, but they still have to come in and make the plays."

Starting at the Packers' 18 with 1:42 to play, Favre drove the Packers 69 yards in 10 plays, including four completions before a 12-yard scramble to the 49ers 13-yard line that ended in a pounding from linebacker Ken Norton Jr. Nonetheless, the woozy Favre regained his senses during a timeout and went straight back to the huddle.

"That's one of the things that makes him so great," said Packers tight end Mark Chmura. "He's so durable. When other guys might get knocked out, he just keeps getting right back up and he keeps making plays."

Unlike the 49ers, who had just cautiously ran the ball and settled for three points and a 20-17 lead, Favre was gunning for the end zone and the win on his last three throws. This, despite already being in field goal range and void of timeouts. A sack or a completion in bounds, and the game is over.

"You know he always does what I tell him to," said Holmgren with a smirk on his face. "He knew he had to throw the ball into the end zone."

"We were trying to score," Beebe said. "We wanted to win the game right then."

His last three attempts, however, went incomplete. And with each throw Favre took more shots from San Francisco defenders.

Jacke then hit the tying field goal.

Favre called the game the most physically demanding he'd ever played in.

"There were some big licks out there," he said.

Added Holmgren: "Brett's pretty beat up. He's exhausted. He gave it everything he had."

He may have been sore, but Favre said he was never tired — even after throwing a team-record 61 passes. He finished 28 of 61 for 395 yards.

"We threw so many times, we had to get something," Favre said. "But we don't want to have to do that."

For the first time this year, Favre completed fewer than 50 percent of his passes. It also was the first game in which he had more interceptions (two) than touchdowns (one).

"Our plays have worked against every other team," he said. "They didn't work tonight."

A big part of Favre's struggles came as a result of the 49ers' interior pass rush, which often collapsed the pocket on Favre. San Francisco quarterback Elvis Grbac faced the same.

"These were two of the best defenses you'll ever see," Favre said of both pass rushes.

One Favre throw in particular seemed to seal the Packers' fate. It came with the score 17-17 and 2:13 to play. Favre threw for rookie receiver Derrick Mayes, but 49ers cornerback Marquez Pope stepped in front of Mayes and made an interception at the Green Bay 24. He returned it 12 yards, setting up the go-ahead field goal for the 49ers.

"I said, 'I guess it's over,' " Favre admitted.

But Favre changed his mind in no time, directing the Packers for the tie.

"I don't want to be known as the Comeback Kid. I'd much rather be ahead," said Favre, who last ran a successful two-minute comeback effort against Atlanta in Milwaukee in 1994 with the playoffs on the line.

Green Bay fans of all types turned out for the San Francisco game.

Beebe Speeds Into the Spotlight

By Chris Havel

Green Bay Press-Gazette

Don Beebe has had big games before, but he has never enjoyed one as much as the Packers' 23-20 victory over San Francisco on Monday night.

The Packers' fastest player became an overnight sensation by catching 11 passes for 220 yards and a touchdown. He had two catches for 20 yards to set up Chris Jacke's 31-yard field goal to tie the game at 20-all in the fourth quarter.

Then, Beebe hauled in a 13-yard reception to help set up Jacke's 53-yard game winner with 11:19 to play in overtime.

The victory moves the Packers, 6-1, into sole possession of first place in the N.F.C. Central after the Vikings' 24-13 loss at Tampa Bay on Sunday. It also moved Beebe into the Packers' record books.

The receiver's 220 yards is third-best in team history behind Billy Howton, who had 257 yards vs. the Rams on Oct. 21, 1956, and Don Hutson, who had 237 yards vs. Brooklyn, on Nov. 21, 1943.

"I had four touchdowns in a game when I was with Buffalo, but we blew Pittsburgh out," he said. "So the way we won this game made it much more enjoyable to help out the team."

Beebe, 31, came into the game when Robert Brooks injured his knee on the Packers' first offensive play from scrimmage. He went on to post the team's first 200-yard receiving game since James Lofton had 206 in a blizzard at Denver on Oct. 15, 1984.

"The little guy can play, can't he?" Packers coach Mike Holmgren said. "What a great effort. We needed it."

Beebe's biggest play, perhaps, came midway through the third quarter when he made a diving catch at the 49ers' 30-yard line, got up and ran untouched into the end zone for a 59-yard touchdown.

The 49ers argued that Merton Hanks had touched Beebe when he was down, and replays showed they were right. But Beebe wasn't going to wait around for a referee's whistle. He got up and got into the end zone.

"I felt something touch me but I wasn't sure if I was down yet," Beebe said. "So that's why I got up and ran. It was just instinct. If you don't feel anybody touched you, you're going to get up and try to get more yardage."

Nobody was going to catch Beebe, who ran the 40-yard dash in 4.25 seconds this past offseason.

"He can scoot," Packers tight end Mark Chmura said. "He's almost as fast as I am."

Running back Edgar Bennett described Beebe's performance as "big-time."

"He's a veteran who got an opportunity and made the most of it," he said.

Beebe, of course, would've preferred it not come at Brooks' expense. Brooks, the team's starting flanker and primary receiver, will be out for the season.

"I don't think I've ever felt so bad for a guy as (Brooks)," Beebe said. "It makes my heart hurt to see him hurt. Sure, it gives me an opportunity. But if I could change things, I would. I'd rather have Robert Brooks in there."

Brooks' injury likely means Beebe will now start at split end opposite Antonio Freeman, who took over for Brooks at flanker. Desmond Howard, who

Don Beebe (82) had a career-day against the 49ers with 11 receptions and 220 yards.

caught four passes for 30 yards, is the third wideout.

Rookie Derrick Mayes, who made his first N.F.L. catch on Monday night, will have the upcoming bye week to make a bid for more playing time. Terry Mickens — the team's No. 3 receiver before being injured in training camp — should return after the bye.

Meantime, Beebe will be hard-pressed to move out of the lineup, especially after Monday night's performance.

"I think from the Packers' standpoint, if you want to be the best, you've got to beat the best," Beebe said. "And that's the way we felt going into this game. We didn't want to make last year's game (a Jan. 6 playoff win over the 49ers) a fluke. Especially not in our backyard."

The Writers

CHRIS HAVEL   Sports columnist and professional football beat writer, *Green Bay Press-Gazette.*

BUD LEA   Retired sports editor of *The Milwaukee Sentinel* and columnist for *Packer Plus.*

THOMAS GEORGE   Professional football beat writer, *The New York Times.*

MICHAEL BAUMAN   Sports columnist, *The Milwaukee Journal Sentinel.*

PETE DOUGHERTY   Professional football beat writer, *Green Bay Press-Gazette.*

BRAD ZIMANEK   Feature writer, *Packer Plus.*

TOM SILVERSTEIN   Professional football beat writer, *The Milwaukee Journal Sentinel.*

Photo Credits